From my Land to the Planet

via Nizza, 56
00198 Roma
www.contrastobooks.com

Original edition
DE MA TERRE A LA TERRE

Photographs and text

Translation: Ruth Taylor
Layout: Tania Russo
Quality check: Barbara Barattolo

ISBN: 978-88-6965-537-1

Sebastião Salgado

with Isabelle Francq

From my Land to the Planet

contrasto

Index

Preface

To look at a photograph by Sebastião Salgado is to experience human dignity, to comprehend what it means to be a woman, a man, a child. Sebastião undeniably nurtures a deep affection for the people he photographs. Otherwise, how could we feel them to be so close, alive and trusting? How could we explain that sense of fraternity as we look at them? For a long time, I have found his work deeply moving. I love the flamboyant aesthetic of his images, their constantly extraordinary light, the power they transmit, but also the tenderness they emanate, which brings me back to the best in myself.

The coincidences of life gave me the chance to meet Sebastião and his wife Lélia. I am enchanted by this pair because, behind Sebastião's international reputation, lies the success story of a rare couple. A story of love and hard work, in which each has his own role to play, his own place and knows exactly what he owes to the other. Together they have built a family, established their own agency, Amazonas Images, they have created Instituto Terra, an environmental project to replant the forest of Brazil's Atlantic coastline, to which they devote the majority of the income deriving from his work and the sale of prints from his collections.

I realized that while Sebastião's images have travelled all over the world, little was known of his own story and the political, ethical and existential roots of his photographic commitment. I wanted to remedy this, to give Sebastião a voice through my journalist's pen. He was kind enough to agree, the day before the presentation of his *Genesis* project—a series of reportages devoted to protected sites on the planet. Between one flight and another, one reportage and another, and despite preparing two books and the openings of his exhibition all over the world, he placed himself at my disposal. With a kindness and simplicity that were disarming, he retraced his journey for me, laying bare his beliefs, allowing me to share his sentiments. It was an enormous pleasure to listen to him and I would now like to share his skill as a raconteur. It is the authenticity of a man who knows how to combine activism and professionalism, talent and generosity.

Isabelle Francq

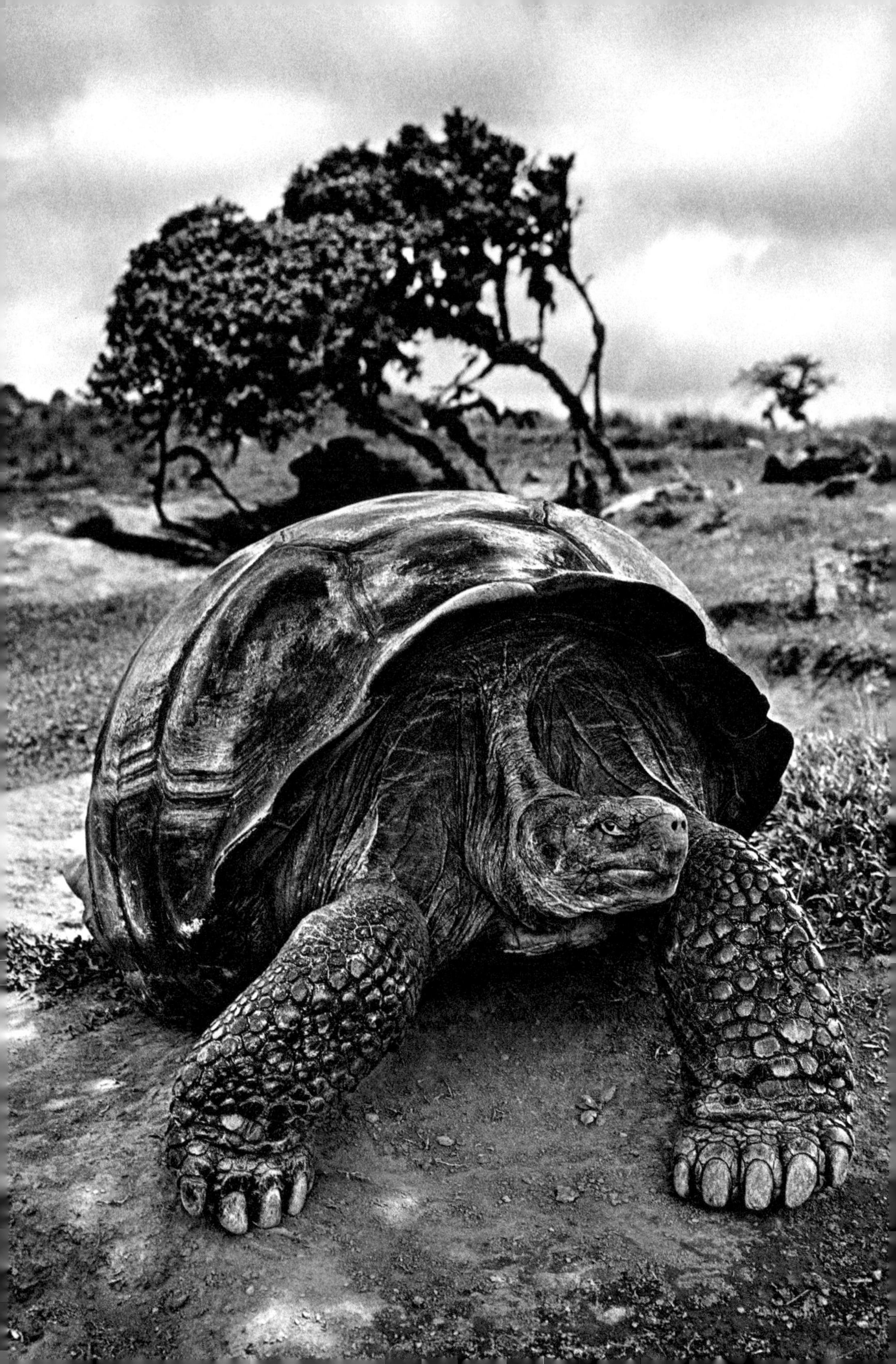

In the beginning: *Genesis*

If you don't like to wait, you can't be a photographer. Once, I arrived on Isabela Island, in the Galápagos, beside a magnificent volcano called Alcedo. This was in 2004. There was a giant tortoise, an enormous creature weighing at least two hundred kilos: one of those who gave the archipelago its name. Every time I approached, the tortoise moved away and although it wasn't walking fast, I could never manage to photograph it.

So I started to think and told myself that when I photograph human beings, I never land in the middle of a group *incognito*, I am always introduced. Then I introduce myself to everyone, I explain, I talk and, gradually, we get to know each other. I realized that, in the same fashion, the only way in which I was going to photograph this tortoise was to get to know it, to get onto its wavelength. So I began to imitate its behaviour: I crouched down and began to move at its height, hands and knees on the ground. From that moment onwards, the tortoise no longer moved away.

As soon as it halted, I immediately took a step backwards. The tortoise came towards me, I moved back again. I waited a few moments, and then gradually I approached, slowly. The tortoise took another step towards me, and I took another one backwards. Then it came towards me again and calmly let me look at it. Then I was able to start photographing. Getting this tortoise to come close took a whole day. A whole day to make it understand that I respected its territory.

Giant tortoise.
Isabela Island,
Galápagos,
Ecuador, 2004

I have realized several photographic essays in my life, reportages that narrate our times and our changing world.

Each one has taken me several years to complete. It is often said that photographers are hunters of images. It's true, we're like hunters who spend a lot of time watching game, waiting for it to emerge from its lair. Taking photographs is the same thing: you have to be patient and wait for something to happen. Because, inevitably something will happen. So you have to learn to savour patience.

Before *Genesis*, I had photographed only one species: humans. During the eight years I have travelled the world for this project dedicated to protected environments, I have learnt to work with other species. From the very first day of my first reportage, thanks to that giant tortoise, I understood that in order to photograph an animal, you have to love it, experience pleasure observing its beauty, its shape. You have to respect it, come into contact with it gradually, preserve its space and its well-being, your way of looking and photographing it. With this knowledge, I began to work with other species just as I have always worked with us human beings.

To begin this series of reportages, having read *The Voyage of the Beagle*,[1] I wanted to retrace Darwin's steps. I spent three months in the Galápagos, which Darwin had reached after having been all round the world and where he completed his theory of evolution. The archipelago, consisting of forty-eight islands and several rocks, is a sort of synthesis of the planet. Some species that live there, like the tortoises, originated from the South American continent, about a

1. *The Voyage of the Beagle*, published in 1839, is one of the titles of the book by Charles Darwin, which was to make him famous.

thousand kilometres away. They arrived there after drifting in the Pacific on the trunks of trees that had been uprooted by the rains. There are eleven different species of tortoise alone, present on some of the islands in the archipelago and not on others. They have evolved in different ways from one island to another. In some places, their backs are completely flattened, perhaps because they lived for hundreds of years under great pressure. Elsewhere, their backs are rounded. I saw some with necks measuring twenty centimetres, while in others it can even reach a metre, probably because, in order to survive on these more or less arid islands, they had to learn to grab hold of leaves at different heights. Nevertheless, these tortoises are all members of the same species.

Like Darwin, I also saw iguanas. On the South American continent, they are terrestrial animals. On the Galápagos, they swim and dive. Again, Darwin understood that it was the aridness of the environment that had forced them to learn to swim. They are, however, cold-blooded creatures: if they remain too long in a place at low temperature, they get cold and die. Many probably died when they reached the Galápagos, diving into the water to drink. Then they learnt to get out in time and to warm themselves in the sun. They also learnt to drink the seawater and developed a small gland above the nose, through which they spit the salt from the water. Like Darwin, I observed all of this—and I am sure that we both saw some of the tortoises I encountered, true "authorities", since these creatures live for more or less two hundred years.

During this voyage, I understood something that was subsequently to serve me throughout the entire *Genesis* project. I discovered that for my whole life I had been told a lie, namely that we are the only rational species. But every species has its own rationality; the problem is to understand it, and this takes time. On the Galápagos, with the exception of the tortoises, animals are not afraid because they have never been hunted by man, and therefore they have no reason to be mistrustful. The tortoises, on the other hand, have never forgotten that in the eighteenth and nineteenth centuries they were hunted by the crews of the ships that stopped in the archipelago, en route to the New World or returning to Europe. These creatures were capable of surviving without food or drink for several months, so by storing them alive in the hold, the sailors were able to guarantee themselves a cargo of fresh meat. That is why, two centuries later, the tortoises are still difficult to approach. It was no coincidence that it took a whole day for the one that I photographed to accept me. There was nothing irrational in its attempts to escape, on the contrary, they were proof of a cautiousness that was entirely conscious. For several generations, species transmit in their genes the warnings of danger related to their predators. And the only predator these giant tortoises have is man; falcons and other birds of prey might attack their young, but the adults are not at risk.

In their own way, the Northern gannets also proved that their behaviour was much more subtle than originally thought, because they don't just act instinctively. One day, we reached Vicente Roca Point on Isabela Island during the mating season. It was extraordinary! I remained for two or three days in the middle of a colony and observed these birds. It is the female who chooses her mate. Four or five males come up to her, one after another they display themselves, spreading their wings, dancing. When the female decides to follow one of them, they fly off together, flying around for ten, fifteen minutes before landing. Another arrives, presents himself, puts on his display, the female flies off with him. And so on. Four or five males court her in a

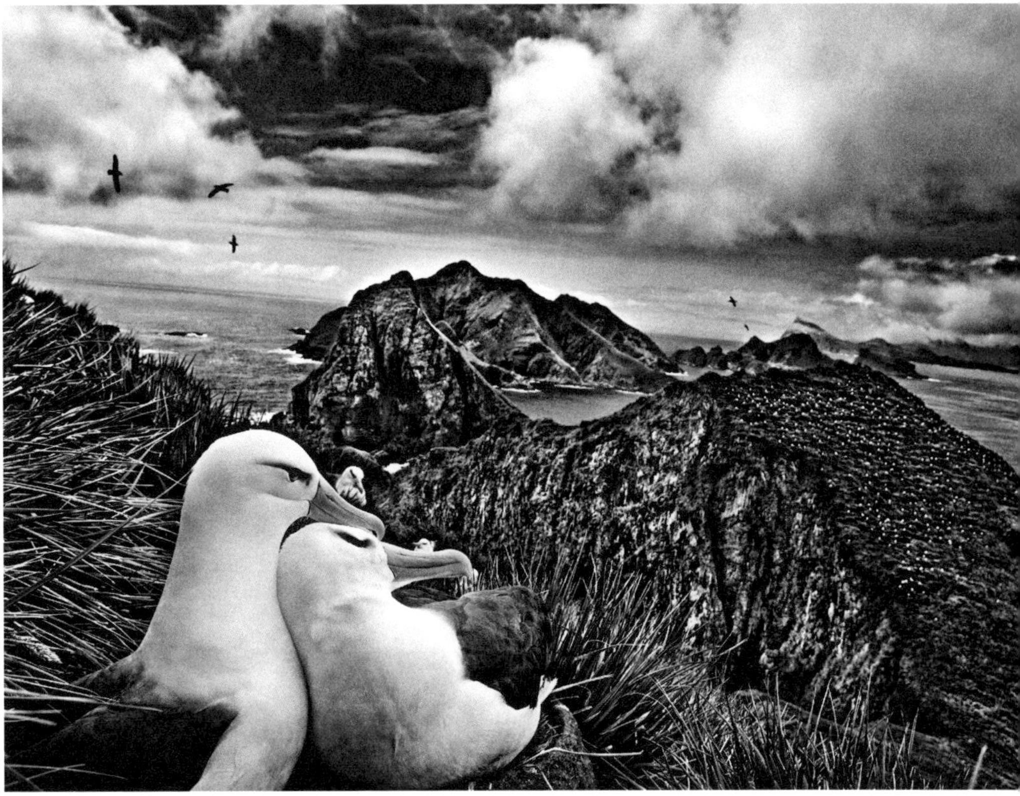

Colony of black-browed albatross. South Georgia, 2009

game that lasts for a couple of hours, then the female finally chooses one of her suitors: he, and he alone, will be her mate for the season, the male with whom she has decided to have her young.

For the albatrosses, the mating season falls at a different time. When I arrived, the young were taking their first flying lessons. They are beautiful birds who fly well, but they land badly, just as they have difficulty taking off. They need a runway, they run, and run, and run… and sometimes fail to take off completely. Really amusing! But to my great surprise, I also discovered the albatrosses are faithful: they find a mate and remain together for life. One day, I saw a male dancing in front of a female. He turned, turned again, spread his wings, and then she began to turn too. They touched each other with the tips of their wings, their beaks, and then suddenly the male flew off. My guide explained: "He's just discovered he's made a mistake. That's not his girlfriend!" This is the sort of scene, incredible *a priori*, one sees when one takes the time to observe animals. This is what I discovered while starting *Genesis* on the Galápagos, and never ceased to experience in the course of all these reportages. Let no one ever tell me that animals are beasts without brain and without logic.

I did not create these reportages as a zoologist or a journalist might have done. I created them for myself, to discover the planet. And I derived enormous pleasure from this. With its minerals, plants, animals, our planet is alive in every way. I realized that this calls for enormous respect on our part.

Genesis was born following on from an environmental project that I set up in Brazil with Lélia Deluiz Wanick Salgado, my wife, my companion and my partner in everything in life. Named Instituto Terra, this project aims to replant the *mata atlântica*,[2] the Atlantic Forest, whose destruction began with the arrival of the Portuguese in 1500. Over the last few decades, following the modernization of the country, deforestation has rapidly increased due to intensive farming, urbanization and, finally, industrialization. Nowadays, only 7% of the original area remains. We have therefore undertaken a restoration of the ecosystem on the land where I

2. Two types of forest co-exist in Brazil: the Atlantic forest, subject to the influence of the ocean, and the Amazon rainforest, which is equatorial.

spent my childhood. Land that we inherited from our parents in the Nineties. Land that deforestation had rendered empty and barren, while I had always had the feeling of growing up in a paradise.

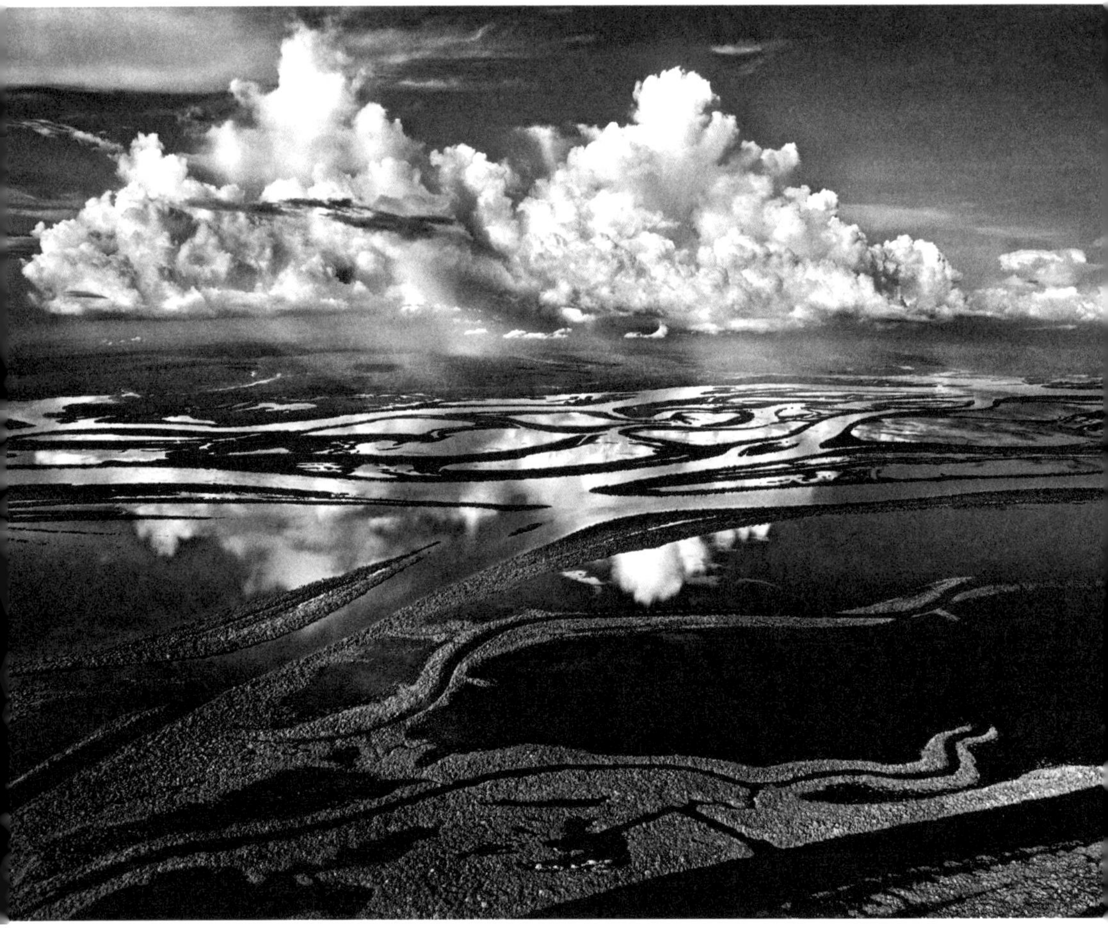

Anavilhanas Archipelago, consisting of about 350 densely forested islands on the Rio Negro. Amazonas State, Brazil, 2009

My homeland

I was born in 1944 in the State of Minas Gerais, on a farm situated in a vast valley called Rio Doce, from the name of the river that waters it. The valley is as big as Portugal, and famous for its gold and iron mines. During my childhood, it was half covered by Atlantic forest. But that was before Brazil entered a market economy and began, like everywhere else, to destroy the forest.

My father's farm was large and self-sufficient, thirty or so families lived there. We produced rice, corn, tomatoes, potatoes and sweet potatoes, fruit and a little milk. And we raised pigs and cattle. It worked well. My father was the owner and he had employees, but all of them owned their own animals and cultivated a bit of land to feed their family. A portion of what they produced went to my father and they kept the rest. No one was rich, no one was poor: this kind of farm had existed in Brazil since the arrival of the Portuguese.

I have wonderful childhood memories of this land. I played in spaces that were immense, there was water everywhere. I swam in rivers, full of caimans—which don't attack man, contrary to popular belief. I had a horse that I rode out on every morning, never coming back until evening. It was a hilly area and I galloped to the boundaries of the farm, to the highest point, and from there, I could look right down the valley. I dreamt of seeing further, I tried to imagine what lay beyond the horizon. We were connected to the rest of Brazil by a railway run by the Vale do Rio Doce company.

Sometimes, during the rainy season, there were landslides and we remained isolated for a month. But we were self-sufficient, we lacked nothing. My childhood remains for me a wonderful time and I still have enormous love for this land.

The photographic projects that I carry out, each one lasting several years and in different places across the planet, might seem very ambitious. Some say that Salgado is a megalomaniac. But I was born in a country that is immense. With its 8,511,965 square kilometres, Brazil covers an area fifteen times that of France. I am used to huge spaces and to travelling: to sleeping one night in one place, and the next in another. When I was very young, my parents let me visit my older sisters who were already married. Alone, I travelled distances equivalent to those from Paris to Moscow or to Lisbon. Communication wasn't easy, part of the journey was on foot, so I learned to travel very young. Nevertheless, it took forty-five days to take the cattle from my father's farm to the abattoir a few hundred kilometres away, winding through farms, forests and streams.

With a few companions, my father made this journey on foot. He drove 500 or 600 pigs with a small stick, and it took him over fifty days to cover the distance. The men had time to talk, to look at the landscape. This slowness is also part of photography. Although the aeroplane, car or train take us rapidly from one part of the globe to another, at the moment you are taking a shot, you have to take your time. You have to adapt to the speed of human beings, animals, life. Even though our world now moves very fast, life is not on this scale. To take photos, you have to respect it.

Once or twice I followed one of those great migrations, but on horseback, behind thousands of cattle. There were no roads, we stopped every twenty kilometres or so in what were known as *estaçóes*, "stations", because the animals could walk no further. Every morning, four or five mules set off before us, carrying the utensils and the canvas sheets that were hung from branches in the evening to create a makeshift kitchen. Dinner was light, with cheeses my mother knew how to prepare well, and some cakes. But at four in the morning, when we woke up, we ate *feijáo tropeiro*, a traditional dish consisting of beans and salted meat that keep well on a journey. This was our main meal of the day. Then, along the way, we gathered bananas or oranges.

My land is extremely beautiful. The mountains are not very high but magnificent nevertheless. If a superior being did create the world, it is here that he must have completed his task, because this land is truly beautiful, so different to anything I have seen elsewhere. Unique.

Here I learnt to see and love the different light that has followed me all my life. In the rainy season, when a storm is brewing, and here they are phenomenal, the sky is full of clouds. I was born with images of heavy skies, pierced by light. These lights have entered my images. In fact, I was inside my images long before I began to make them. I also grew up with contre-jour: as a child, to protect my fair skin, I was always forced to wear a hat, or else to sit under a tree, because at that time there were no sunscreens. Also, I always saw my father coming towards me from the sunlight, contre-jour. And so this light, these expanses of land are my history. I am the product of these places, these journeys and these different lights. And now that I live in France, whenever I have to go to America or China, they feel less far away than the distance from our farm to the abattoir.

When I was 15, I left Aimorés, the little town of 12,000 inhabitants close to my father's farm, where I went to school. I went to Vitória, in the state of Espírito Santo, to complete my secondary school education. There, I discovered a different planet. For example, I had never seen a telephone, because they didn't exist in my town. We simply listened to the shortwave radio, when it worked, except during the rainy season. So we were unable to follow the news in a continuous way.

I belong to the first generation who left the countryside to study in the town. Before becoming a farmer, my father had been a pharmacist, but he had never followed any classes. At the beginning of the 1930s, he had taken part in a revolution. As his political faction lost, he had left with my mother to begin a new life in the state of Minas Gerais. Before acquiring the farm, he had initially bought a dozen mules and had set himself up in the transportation business, of coffee in particular. With the mules laden with sacks, he walked for twelve days through the forest, from the plantations to the train station in Aimorés. Just like his father, my grandfather, a wholesaler and adventurer who adored travelling and discovering new places. He died of malaria in a region far from home, two or three months' journey away at that time. His family learnt of his death two or three years later. But everyone of my generation who comes from Brazil's inland has similar stories to tell.

In Vitória, I lived with five or six other boys of my age. We took it in turns to manage the collective budget for a month. So when I was young, I learnt a bit about managing money. I also had to find myself a little job, because although my father had a large farm, he reinvested a large

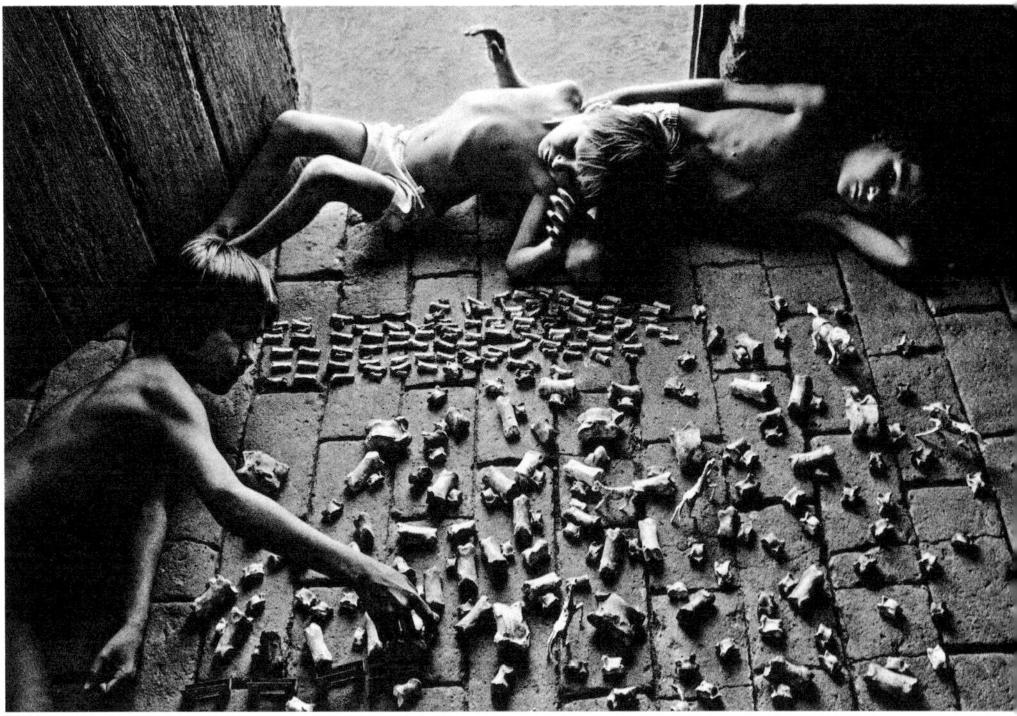

Brazil, 1983

portion of what it produced and so he didn't have much money. I worked in the secretariat of the Alliance française, in the accounts department. Here again, I had to deal with figures. My father longed for me to become a farmer like him, or else a lawyer, so after my secondary studies, I enrolled at the faculty of law. I liked the historical part, but didn't enjoy the rest at all.

At that time, the country's economy was starting to change. The first car factories appeared towards the end of the 1950s. Juscelino Kubitschek, the Brazilian president who was to remain in office from 1956 until 1961, was probably the most dynamic supporter of development that the country has ever known. He built Brasilia, founded on the

21st of April 1960. Thanks to him, Brazil began to awaken from a long sleep lasted four hundred years and we had the feeling of living in a new country. Like many young people, I wanted to be part of this movement. Law seemed so traditional to me, while economics seemed to represent, in my view, everything that was most modern. At that time SUDENE (The Superintendency for the Development of the Northeast) and ALALC (The Latin American Free Trade Association) were created and faculties of economics were established. I wanted to become an economist: I was keen to embark on this modern adventure.

At the Alliance française, when I was 20 years old, I fell in love with Lélia, a student who was 17 and enrolled in fifth year. Lélia was born in Vitória and had studied piano at the music academy for ten years. At the age of 17, she had begun to work as a primary school teacher, giving piano lessons at the same time. She was wonderful. We have been married for more than forty-five years, and I still find her as beautiful as she was then. Ever since we met, we have shared everything. Together, we discovered politics when we were still kids.

The group I lived with followed closely the development of the situation in the country. We watched people leave the countryside and migrate towards the towns. Industry needed labour, so entire families left. We witnessed the emergence of social inequalities. I had been unaware of them until then. I came from a world that operated outside any system of market economy, in which there were neither rich nor poor. Just as on my father's farm, everyone had sufficient means to house, feed, dress and support his family. With the industrial system, people coming from the countryside discovered an entirely different life in the cities, and the majority fell into poverty. I began to frequent comrades who were active in left-wing parties; the Communist Party was very active at the time. Some belonged to associations such as the Catholic Student Youth. These left-wing Christian institutions gave rise to parties that were much more radical, like Ação Popular (Popular Action) to which I belonged. This group adhered to Cuban ideals and was open to armed struggle.

When I started university, the study of economics, compared to the present, was very different: now they pre-eminently focus on business economics. This was part of our course, but it included above all political economics, macroeconomics, public finance. I was really interested in macro accounting. I wanted to work on long term projects, on economic models in which, if certain variables were controlled, it was possible to give impulse to a true economic trend. I was especially interested in the idea of large-scale saving, and wanted to continue my studies with a Masters degree at the University of São Paulo. This degree had just been set up, it was unique in Brazil, and there were only twenty-five posts available. I was lucky enough to be accepted and to win a scholarship. I received my first degree on the 15th of December 1967. Lélia and I were married on the 16th and we left immediately for São Paulo so that I could begin my Masters degree in January. I was twenty-three, she was twenty-one.

Some of our lecturers came from American universities, and I was even taught by the Brazilian minister of Finance, as well as the President of the Central Bank of Brazil. The aim of the course was to create a group of middle managers capable of responding to the enormous needs of the country, and I had the privilege of being part of it.

On the 31st of March 1964, a coup led by Marshal Castelo Branco overthrew President João Goulart and, consequently, the Second Republic. A military regime was established and remained in power until the election of Tancredo Neves, in 1985. The military justified their coup d'état, which occurred a few years after the Cuban regime's alignment with the USSR, on the pretext of the threat of communism. There was an enormous popular protest movement against this dictatorship and against all the violations of human rights in which it engaged. A great opposition movement also arose against the United States' interference in Latin America, through the CIA, under the pretext of keeping order. In this new climate, the revolutionary sentiment was such that Lélia and my commitment became radicalized still further. We took part in all the protests and in all the acts of resistance to the regime, and together with our comrades, we were absolutely determined to defend our ideals. It was very dangerous of course. Our group decided that the younger members, including us, should leave and regroup abroad, continuing to operate from outside, while those who were older were to go into hiding.

Just before our departure in the summer of 1969, between May and June, Lélia lost her mother, who died of cancer, and her father, who lost his life in a fire. Huge drama in our lives. In just two months, Lélia had become an orphan. She was barely twenty years old. In August, we left our country. When we boarded the ship, we knew that if we were discovered, we would be thrown into prison and tortured. I remember our relief on leaving the last port, when the ship finally headed away from the coast of Brazil towards France.

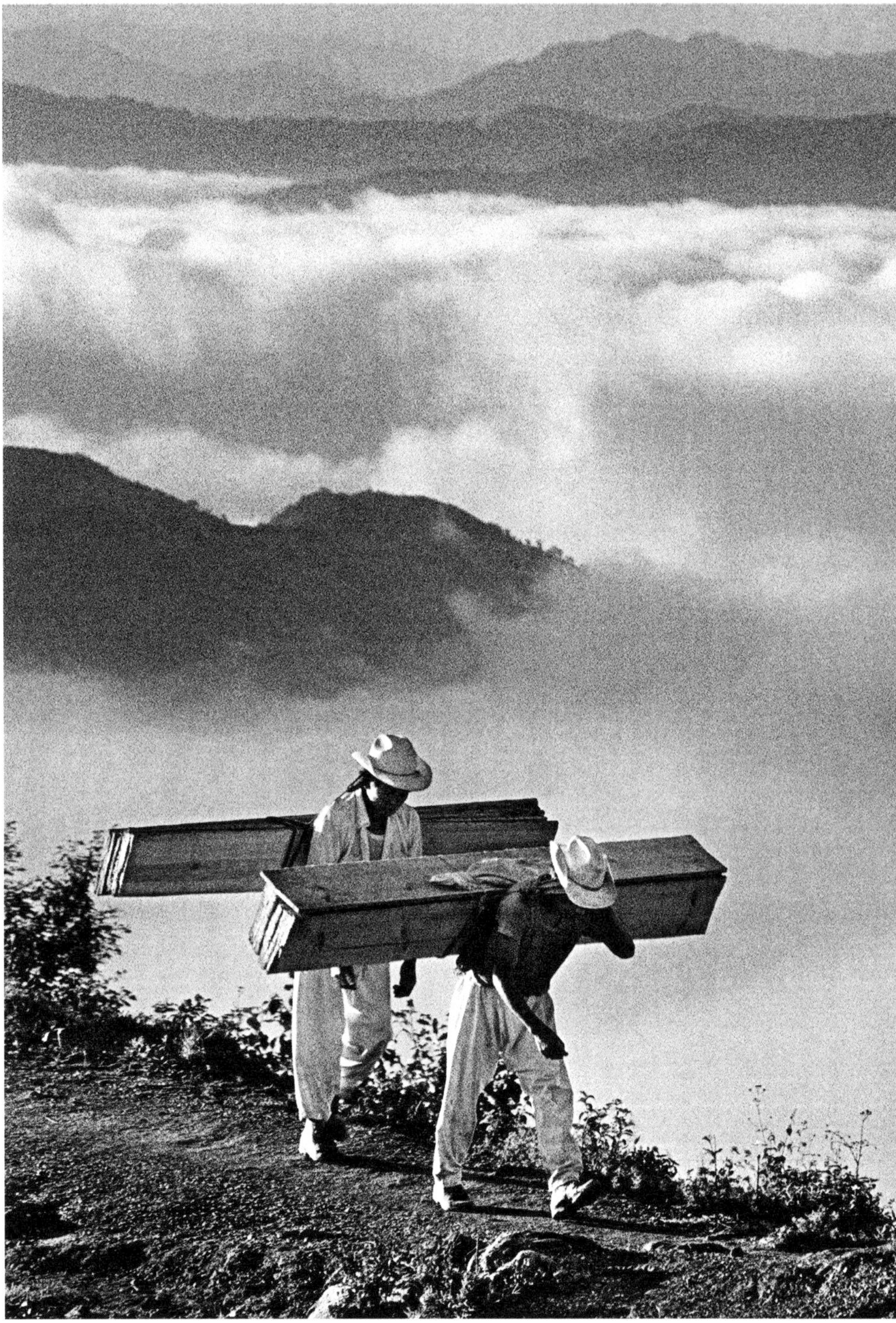

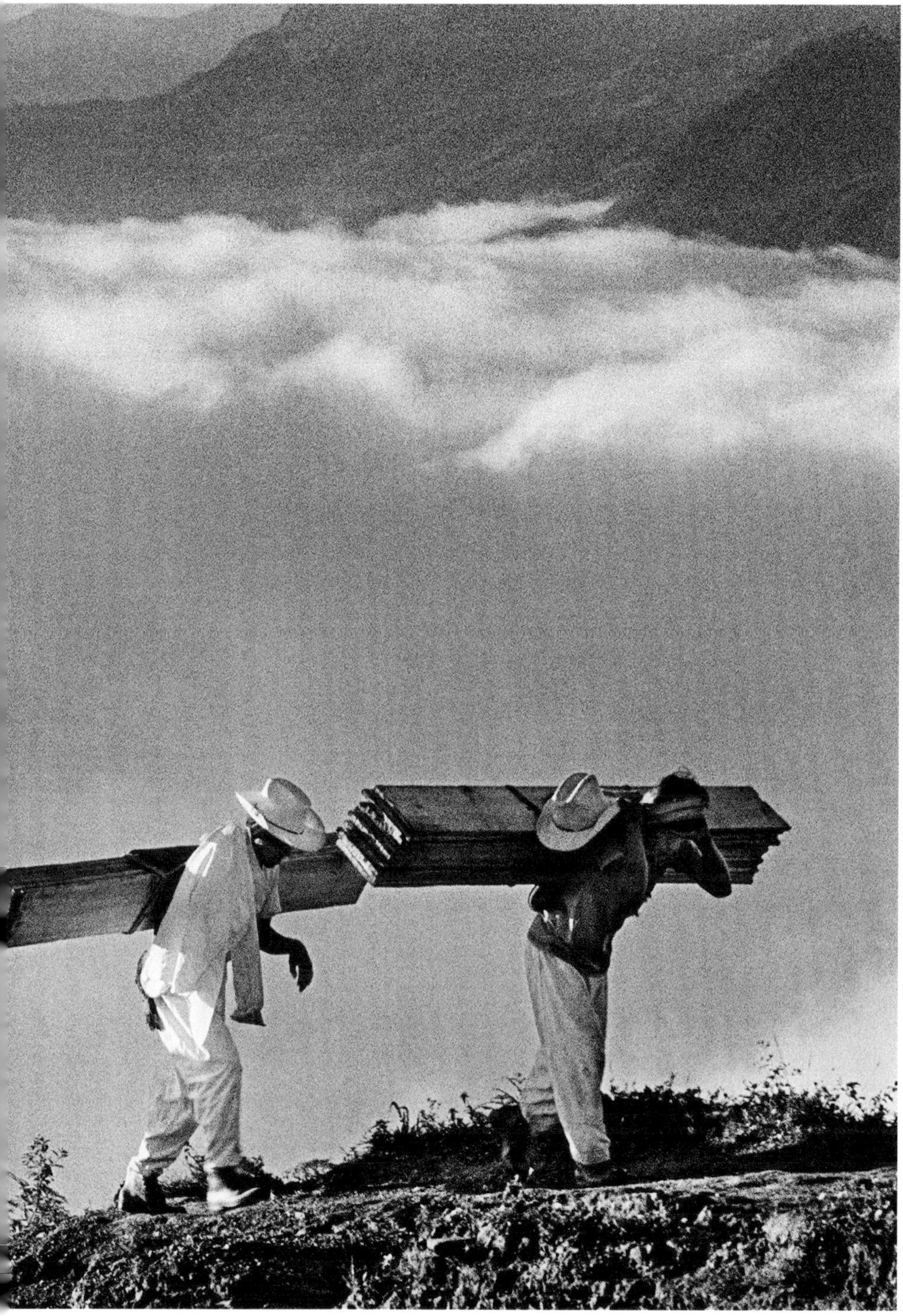

Mexico, 1980

In France and not elsewhere

For Lélia and I, going to France was fantastic. Most French people are unaware of it, but Brazilians adore France. From the end of the nineteenth century, all our intellectuals have spent time there, and the first Brazilian Constitution was inspired by French Republican principles. Every Brazilian town with a population of over a hundred thousand inhabitants had its Alliance française, with its own French director. In Brazil, we started to study French at the same time as Latin, at the beginning of secondary school. Learning English did not happen until two years later. In Vitória, as I have already mentioned, I occupied the position of secretary at the Alliance française, under the supervision of our life-long friends Juju and Pierre Merigoux. Juju comes from Juiz de Fora (Minas Gerais) and Pierre is from Limoges. A map of Paris lay open under the glass on top of my desk. So when I arrived in France, I knew exactly where to find Boulevard Raspail, Rue de Rivoli and Place de la Bastille. It was also at the Alliance française that I had met Lélia, who already spoke and wrote perfect French.

For us, France was the obvious choice: it was the home of the rights of man and of democracy. It was the third option between communism and the United States. We admired the communists, who were the principal support for the left, but we had doubts about a certain obscurantism they showed. As for the Americans, our trust in them was non-existent: we considered them to be at the origin of the repression that weighed on us. They had never formed an alliance with anything of popular or democratic nature. They always contributed to keeping in office the most powerful and those possessing weapons. France was for us the country of ideals that were democratic, but also economic—it had some excellent economists at the time. Officially, I was also there to study at the ENSAE (The Centre for Research in Economics and Statistics).

We arrived in Paris in August 1969; everything seemed wonderful to us: the long, endless days, the mornings that began so early. But then autumn came, the light decreased and, by December, Lélia and I were on the verge of depression. We missed our own country terribly. We knew we could no longer return home, because we were too involved with the protest movements. We were very young and it was very hard.

In France, Lélia did not play the piano again for many years. Now, she plays again, but only for us. The death of her parents and leaving our country had meant such a break, such suffering that she made the decision to change her life. So when we arrived in Paris, she enrolled at the Ecole des Beaux-Arts to study architecture, while I prepared my PhD. We had no scholarships. We had taken a room at the Cité Universitaire and, in parallel with our studies, had started to work. I unloaded lorries at the Cité Universitaire Co-operative and Lélia worked in the library.

We had arrived with a little money, two thousand dollars, with which we immediately bought a 2CV. We knew Paris, at least in theory, thanks to all we had read over the years. But we wanted to visit the rest of the country. We found France beautiful. Everywhere, from Alsace, to the Pyrenees, to Provence... Brazil covers an area fifteen times that of France, but France is fifteen times more varied than Brazil. Little by little, France became our country. Like Brazil.

In France, we learnt about solidarity and once you have experienced it, you never look back. We were approached by Brazilians who had just arrived, completely destroyed by the dictatorship. Many had been tortured. Leftist organizations managed to help some to escape via Argentina and Uruguay, but when they arrived, they were physical and mental wrecks. At weekends, we made trips around France in our 2CV, trying to raise money for these refugees. On Saturdays, with our Brazilian fellow activists, we set off for Verdun, Metz, and so on. We cooked Brazilian dishes and Lélia sang. We were helped by all the movements of the French left, like the CGT (General Confederation of Labour), the CFDT (French Democratic Confederation of Labour), the Communist Party, the PSU (the Unified Socialist party), as well as by Christian movements like the CCFD (Catholic Committee against Hunger and for Development) and Cimade, an ecumenical organization providing help and support for foreign migrants. In other words, we had arrived knowing nobody, not only were we no longer isolated, but we found ourselves surrounded by a close network of support, governed by a true sense of sharing and mutual assistance, on a material as well as psychological level. We were homesick, but felt welcomed and in return, we tried to support those who were arriving. It was also the period of the repression in Portugal and we felt ourselves involved in the movements against the Salazar dictatorship: as Brazilians, we were close to the Portuguese. But we also felt solidarity with the Poles, Angolans, Guatemalans, Chileans, in other words with all immigrants and illegal immigrants.

We now have evidence that when we arrived in France we were spied on. The Brazilian archives, opened recently, provided us with documents on us by the SNI (National Information Service). We have discovered that, at the time, our lives were under surveillance. People we thought of as friends, who came to our home, reported us. There were descriptions of our house, even that there was a vase of flowers in a particular place in our apartment. Everything was recorded. Even the name of the director of the Gamma Agency for which I had once worked after choosing photography, Jean Monteux, who had helped me in 1976, when the Brazilian government had refused to renew my passport. He had come with me to the consulate to support my application: I needed the passport to carry out my reportages abroad. In the archives, we found evidence of a request by the Brazilian secret services to investigate Jean Monteux, as though Gamma were a centre of subversion, under the pretext that he had offered me his support. That's what a dictatorship is, and how immoral it can be. In the end, I obtained French nationality. But at the same time, together with a friend, Augusto Boal, a Brazilian theatre director who had fled to Portugal and was in the same situation, I had filed a case against the Brazilian Ministry of Foreign Affairs, because it was anti-constitutional to refuse a citizen a passport. We won and this created a precedent—after us, others who were in the same situation also brought cases against the government.

It is a great joy to see all those who were formerly persecuted, tortured and beaten now in power in Brazil. To see that, at last, since President Fernando Henrique Cardoso, Lula's predecessor, it is the left that has brought about change. To see that our companions in the struggle have become ministers and that Lula, who took part in the protest movement without ever leaving the country because he came from the working class, after being arrested and persecuted, has become the greatest president Brazil has ever known. He has managed to raise 35 million Brazilians from living on the poverty line to the middle class. The same goes for President Dilma Rousseff. She was also imprisoned, beaten, tortured. The dictatorship that caused so much suffering fell in the end because, like all dictatorships, it was a regime without a future. On the other hand, weighing everything up, no regime has survived, whether it be fascism, nazism, or the deviated communism of the Soviet Union. It is as if there were a natural order, something greater, driving reality towards a more noble destiny. Proof that justice exists, after all.

One click was enough

Thanks to our support network, as soon as we arrived in Paris we made many friends. In the spring of 1970, the Houssay family lent us a house in the village of Menthonnex-sous-Clermont, near Annecy, so that I could recover. I had fallen ill, my glands were very swollen and for a while it was feared that perhaps I had cancer, until the doctors finally diagnosed my illness: hay-fever. I was in fact experiencing a proper spring for the first time—in Brazil there is nothing like it. We took advantage of our stay in Savoie to take our 2CV to Geneva, where at the time it was possible to acquire photographic equipment for the best prices in Europe: Lélia needed some to photograph buildings.

She chose a Pentax Spotmatic II with a Takumar 50mm, f1:4 lens. We knew nothing about photography, but straightaway we thought this camera was fantastic. When we got back to Menthonnex, we took our first pictures, read the instructions and three days later, we returned to Geneva again to buy two more lenses: a 24mm and a 200mm. This is how photography came into my life. Returning to Paris, I created a small photo lab for myself at the Cité Universitaire.

After a few months, I left my job as a warehouseman at the co-operative and began to make prints for the students, which earned me a little money. Then I carried out my first reportage thanks to the Brazilian writer Jorge Amado[1], when

1. Jorge Amado de Faria (1912-2001) wrote over thirty novels, most notably *Captains of the Sands.*

he was awarded a prize by the Académie française, together with the Portuguese writer Ferreira de Castro. I then received some minor commissions for other reportages. Gradually, I began to think that I could become a photographer. Lélia and I began to dream about buying a Volkswagen campervan, installing a photo lab in it and travelling around Africa. In the meantime, however, I had to finish my doctorate.

In 1971, after completing my postgraduate studies in Paris, I landed myself the most fantastic job in London, with the International Coffee Organization, where I thought I would write the final part of my thesis. In the end, I never did. Nevertheless, I tried to reason with myself, saying repeatedly: "You have to become a serious economist, you have worked hard for it, while photography..." I became an international administrator and, suddenly, I was earning a good salary. Lélia and I bought a sports car, a magnificent Triumph, and we rented a beautiful flat close to Hyde Park. Nevertheless, Lélia kept her room at the Cité Universitaire in Paris, where she continued her studies. We met each other in London after my African trips. I was travelling a lot.

Working in conjunction with the World Bank and FAO, the United Nations Organization for Food and Agriculture, my task was to set up and finance projects for economic development in Africa. I was responsible for Rwanda, Burundi, the Congo, and second in command for Uganda and Kenya. We participated in the introduction of tea growing in Rwanda, with the aim of establishing agricultural diversification in this coffee producing country. The International Coffee Organization had created an investment fund into which each producing country and each consuming one had to deposit the equivalent of a dollar for every sack produced or bought.

This money served to carry out studies to regulate coffee production, in order to avoid exceeding supply demand and a fall in price. I remember my first trip to Africa in 1971. I spent fifty days travelling around Burundi and Rwanda in a Volkswagen Beetle—at that time, there were no surfaced roads in Rwanda—with Joseph Munyankindi, director of the country's Office of Industrial Culture, who was to become a friend.

Together with teams from the World Bank and the FAO, we identified the sites destined to become large tea plantations in the Kivu region, where the soil is particularly fertile and the altitude perfect. In this great coffee-producing nation, we established the first unit of tea production. At that time, I completed a 30-year profitability analysis, a macroeconomic project employing 32,000 families, each one with its own plot of land to cultivate. When I returned there, in 1991, for my photographic project *Workers*, these plantations had become truly magnificent. Although it wasn't the largest producer, Rwanda was then producing the best tea in the world, a much sought-after nectar used to enrich with its aroma other varieties coming from Asia. It obtained the highest prices on the London Exchange.

It was thanks to my work as an economist that I discovered Africa. On this continent, I rediscovered my paradise.

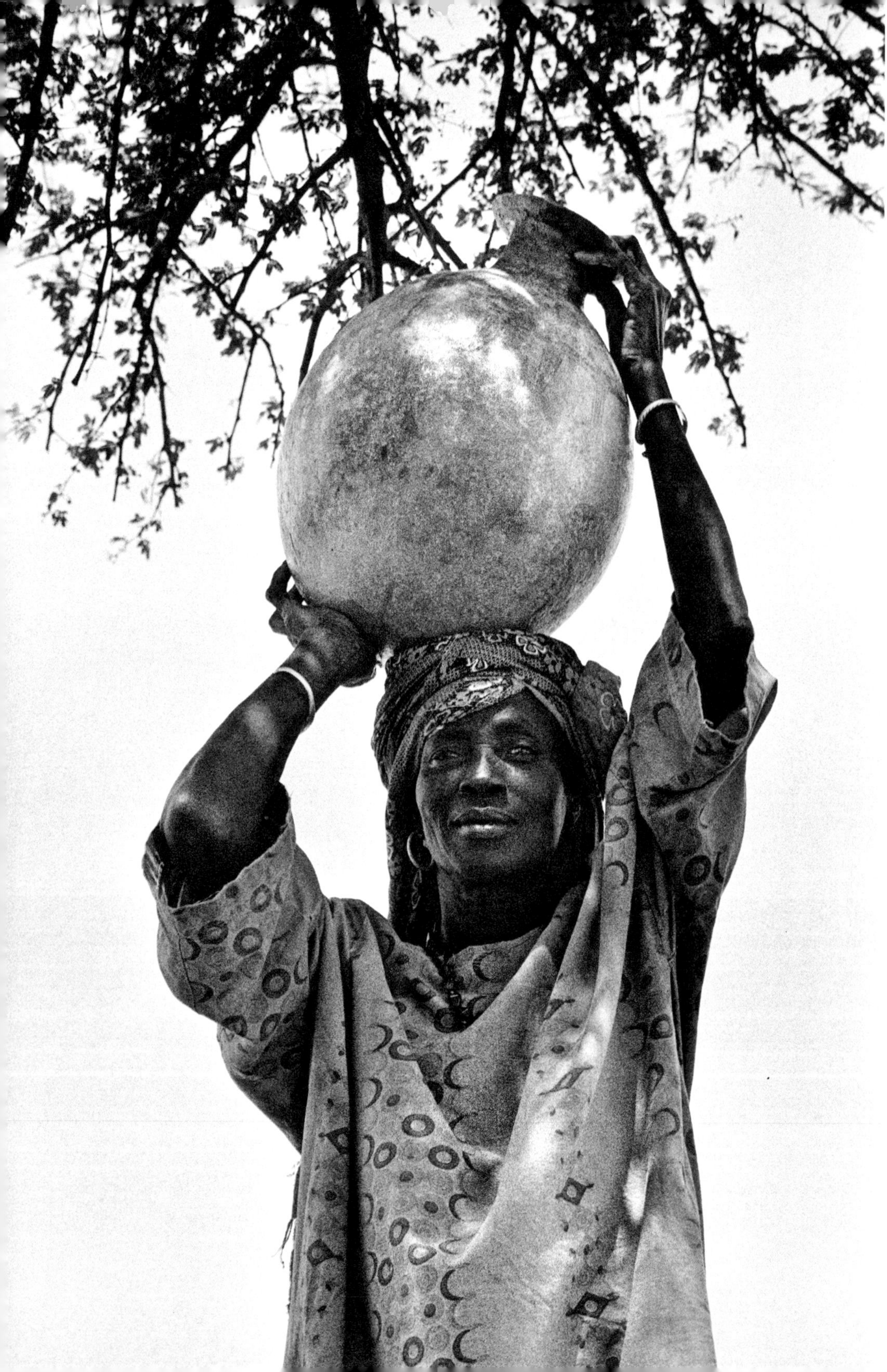

Africa, my other Brazil

Discovering Rwanda was like rediscovering my own country. Africa is the other half of Brazil: looking at the globe, it is obvious that Africa, Latin America and Antarctica were one continent before they were separated, 150 million years ago. Despite the separation of the continents, the same vegetation and minerals are found in Africa and South America. On a cultural level, slaves originating from Mozambique, Guinea, Angola, Benin and Nigeria who were taken to Brazil by the Portuguese, have left a profound mark on society. Fragments of the history and traditions of these peoples form part of what has become Brazilian culture. That is why the influence of Africa is so important to us. I had dreamt of going there ever since I was a child. When I arrived in Rwanda, I immediately felt I was on familiar ground: our ways of life are similar, we have similar ways of eating, talking and enjoying ourselves. Throughout my life, I have gone to Africa as often as I possibly could. My story is completely bound up with this continent.

During the journeys to Rwanda, Burundi, Zaire, Kenya and Uganda, I realized that the photos I was taking made me much happier than the reports that I had to write on my return. I wrote them diligently and the work was undeniably fascinating. But photography…

In London, on Sundays, Lélia and I would hire a boat and go into the middle of the Serpentine, an artificial lake in Hyde Park. We would lie down in the boat and, for hours, discuss my desire to abandon economics for photography. I never ceased to ask myself: shall I do it? Until one day, my

Woman carrying water at Tchin Tabaraden, Tahoua Region, Niger, 1973 desire got the upper hand and I made the decision to give up economics. This was in 1973. I was 29 and, with Lélia's consent, I decided to abandon a promising career to become a freelance photographer.

Gone were the good salary, the beautiful apartment, the sports car. We returned to Paris and rented a *chambre de bonne* that served as a laboratory by day and a bedroom by night. At the time, Lélia was preparing a thesis on urbanism, as well as spending long nights working in architectural practices to support us. In other words, she provided additional support whenever a project was approaching its deadline. Each time, the work was so intense that she lost count of her hours. In addition, she was also working on the preparation of a small paper for Brazilians in Paris. She learnt about making a mock-up, iconography, editing, all of which were to prove useful in the publication of our own books. We invested all our savings in photographic equipment. We had a goal, and because of that, we were prepared to put up with anything. I remember that we didn't have a shower, but lots of friends with homes where we could go to wash!

The same year, we set off to carry out a reportage. In Africa, of course! Lélia was expecting our first child, Juliano, but we travelled across Niger nevertheless. It was summer and the heat was appalling, but we could sense Africa and we loved being there. We had gone there with the CCFD (whose representatives in Niger were Choly and Marcos Guerra, she from Argentina and he from Brazil) and Cimade to photograph the famine. We went to the places in which these organizations had established programmes to combat the drought. We travelled in trucks and planes carrying food supplies. It was hard and we witnessed some terrible scenes, but it was also exhilarating and we sensed that our images would help. There were two of us taking photos: our friend Antonio Luiz Mendes Soares, another young Brazilian, took those in colour, while I was responsible for black and white.

On our return from Niger, we moved to Enghien-les-Bains, to a lovely house belonging to the Bassé family, great friends who had also lent us the money needed for our reportage in Niger. There, we were able to develop the films and print the photos. During this period, I got ill. At the end of the trip, after weeks of eating cassava, I hadn't been able to resist buying some meat in the market at Agadez. It must have been contaminated, and I had contracted toxoplasmosis. Luckily, thanks to the sixth sense that pregnant women have, Lélia had not eaten any. So she had to take charge of contacting magazines and selling the photos. At the time, Lélia was also working in the lab, developing the films, doing the printing, in other words, she participated in everything. The CCFD liked one of my images very much. It showed a woman against the light, by a tree and with a pot on her head and they decided to print it as a poster for the campaign "The planet belongs to everyone". My photo was thus hung in all the churches in France, in all the parish houses and in many CFDT centres. I didn't know how much to ask. The CCFD helped me to set a price that enabled me to earn a significant sum for that time, with which we could have acquired a small apartment. But Lélia and I preferred to invest the money in photographic equipment. I bought all the Leicas[1] I needed, an excellent photo glazing machine and a professional enlarger which we still use.

1. German 24x36 mm, the true Rolls Royce of cameras.

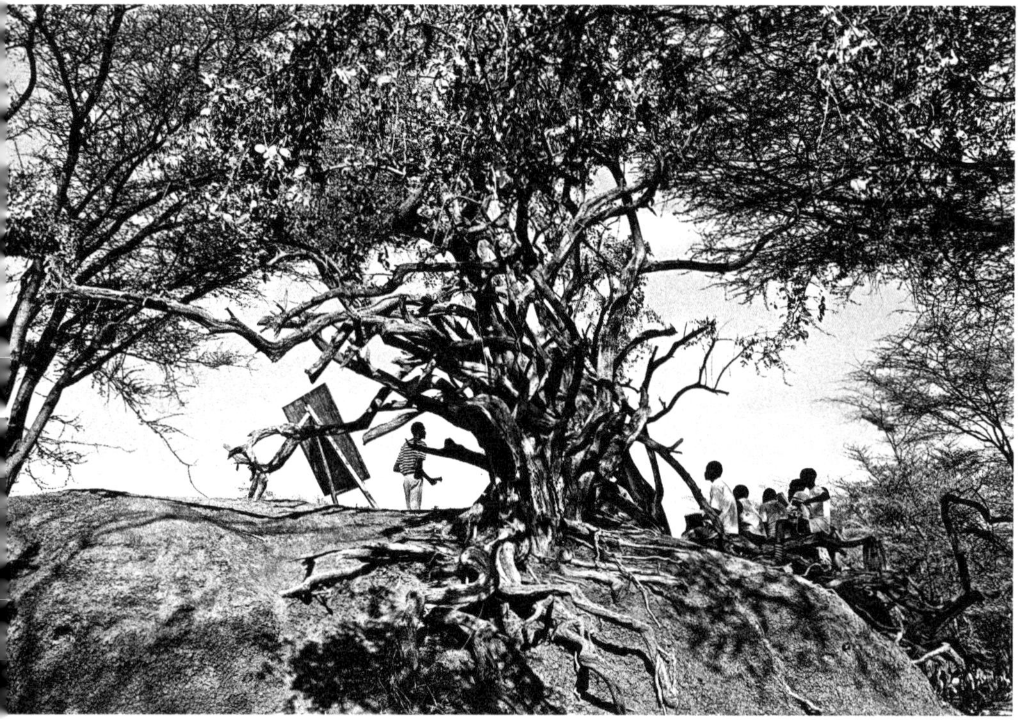

Young men fleeing from Sudan to avoid being recruited into the army, Kenya, 1993

I don't claim to be a specialist on Africa, but I love photographing it. When I was working for Gamma photo agency, from 1975 to 1979, I volunteered to go to Africa at every possible opportunity. I was more interested in long-term stories than in the latest events. At that time, you could earn a very good living taking photos of councils of ministers or portraits of celebrities. My particular niche, however, was not very lucrative: I covered events for which the images were usually published only once, while they were still current news, and then they were consigned to the archives. Nevertheless, my work contributed to supporting our little family, and that made me happy. It paid off in the end: thanks to the forty or so reportages I carried out in Africa over a period of thirty years, I was able to publish my book *Africa* in 2007.

I had so many images of the continent that I was also able to publish a second one. I feel enormously privileged to have been able to travel there so often over the years. In the end, these numerous journeys have given my work consistency, as well as providing opportunities to see and to learn, and allowing me to reveal through my photos the changes that have taken place in these countries.

Ever since I discovered photography, I have never ceased to photograph, and every time I derive enormous pleasure from it. My training as an economist has enabled me to convert this pleasure of the moment into projects that are more long-term.

Young activist, young photographer

When I first threw myself into photography, I was ready to try everything: nudes, sports, portraits. One day, without even knowing how or why, I found myself focusing on social issues. In fact, it was entirely natural. I had been part of that younger generation who, at the beginning of Brazil's great industrialization, had been very concerned about social problems.

Immediately after we arrived in France, while I was still studying economics, Lélia and I wanted to go to the Soviet Union, to perfect our left-wing education. So in 1970, we drove our 2CV to Prague, to visit a friend of Lélia's uncle (her uncle had been one of the founders of the Brazilian Communist party). This friend was a member of the central committee of the Brazilian Communist party who had fled to Czechoslovakia. In Prague, he told us: "Forget the Soviet Union. Here, it's over, bureaucracy has taken the power from the people. If you want to be activists, go and do it in France, with the immigrants". It was a terrible blow. Without ever having belonged to the Communist party, we felt demoralized seeing this man who, having experienced the system from within, had lost his faith in the international communism on which he had founded the hope of creating a better Brazil.

We then decided to go to Leipzig where, at that time, a great gathering of all the communist countries was being organized. As we left Prague, it was snowing, and we discovered how similar it was to driving through mud in Brazil.

In Leipzig, we viewed the showcase of the production of the communist world, and immediately decided to return to Prague. When we reached the border, however, we were not permitted to enter Czechoslovakia a second time. So we found ourselves trapped on the border between two communist countries. The German authorities then gave us a visa to return to Leipzig, but we were held up by the snow for several days on the way. We eventually reached Karl-Marx-Stadt, the city in Saxony renamed Chemnitz in 1990, not far from the border with the West. While we were searching for a hotel, we came across a policeman; two minutes later, we were surrounded by machine guns, pointed at us by thugs with a menacing air. They asked us what we had been up to after almost a week in communist Germany, and subjected us to several interrogation sessions. Fortunately, Lélia eventually found in her bag the hotel receipt proving that we had indeed been in Leipzig. After verifying this, the police ordered us to leave the country by six o'clock the following morning and before the changing of the guard in Berlin, because the officials on the next shift might have decided not to allow us to go. As we had no petrol, they gave us a can for free, and helped us to reach the border as fast as possible. We were then subjected to a thorough search, with mirrors even being used to check underneath the car. Finally, we were able to cross into the West, having gained a taste of what communism was like. We realized that the system that still held for us a certain romanticism, was entirely devoid of any sensitivity or tenderness, just as our friend in Prague had told us and we had found difficult to believe…

When I am asked how I came to social documentary photography, I reply that it is simply an extension of my political commitment and of my roots. We knew many refugees, who, like us, had fled from the dictatorships of South America, but also from Poland, Portugal, Angola… So it was entirely natural that I should have started to photograph refugees and illegal immigrants, firstly in France and then in other European countries. As I have already mentioned, my love for Africa drove me to devote my first great reportage to that continent; it was not its landscapes or its traditions that I wanted to show at the beginning, but the famine that was affecting its people. This was how I began to work alongside the CCFD and Cimade.

Although we are not believers ourselves, Lélia and I felt in tune with social Christianity. My first reportages were published in *Christiane* and *La Vie*. At the time, the Christian press was considered "minor", although it was perhaps more important than the "major press". *La Vie* then had a weekly print-run of over half a million copies, while that of *SOS*, Secours Catholique's monthly magazine, for which I also worked a great deal, was over a million. I also worked with *Croissance des Jeunes Nations*, with Bayard Presse, and published many photos in the magazines produced by the Fleurus group.

All of these papers had an enormous readership; there was a strong Christian movement in France. That was my world: Christians were committed to helping refugees and under-developed countries, and I came from an under-developed country myself. Through photography, I sought to show this exploited world, in all its dignity. Over the years, I have often had occasion to work with UNICEF, Médecins sans Frontiéres, the Red Cross, and the UNHCR (UN High Commissioner for Refugees), among others. In short, I have remained close to the world of humanitarian relief.

While I was working for the International Coffee Organization in Rwanda, I had seen workers toiling for twelve hours a day in the heat of the plantations, barefoot. They had no social security and their salary did not allow them to have decent housing, to look after themselves or to educate their children. They worked as much as, if not more, European workers, but the product of their labour had no value and what they produced was exported at a loss. It was as if they were paying us to consume their coffee, offering us into the bargain their health, their comfort and all their basic needs. I felt the burden of an enormous injustice. Lélia and I came to the conclusion that the world is divided into two, on one side, freedom for those who have everything and, on the other, a lack of everything for those who have nothing. Through my photos, it was this dignified and exploited world that I wished to show to a European society sophisticated enough to receive this appeal.

During my training, I had essentially studied political economy, in other words "quantified sociology". We also studied history and different economic theories, subjects that in the end closely relate to philosophy and the history of ideas. At ENSAE, it was also possible to study econometrics (mathematics applied to economics). In the study group on Marxism to which Lélia and I belonged, we had followed courses on geopolitics by Professor Anouar Abdel Malek from Cairo University, who had also taken refuge in Paris at that time. In other words, I had a solid education. Arriving in a country for the first time, I was able to grasp the situation quickly and to place my images in historical and sociological context. To me, photography is like writing—what writers tell with the pen, I tell with my camera. It is a passion, as I love the light, but also a language that is extremely powerful. When I first took it up, I had no limits.

I wanted to go everywhere my curiosity took me, where beauty moved me. But also everywhere there was social injustice, in order to relate it better.

At that time, I joined Gamma photo agency, the greatest school of photojournalism. I remained there from 1975 until 1979, after spending a year with Sygma. The atmosphere at Gamma was exceptionally friendly. Most of the photographers had arrived recently; there was another group that was more experienced, people who were not necessarily much older, but who, unlike me, had been photographers for a long time: Raymond Depardon, Marie-Laure de Decker, Hugues Vassal and Floris de Bonneville, an excellent news editor. They did not share my left-wing origins, but had their own view of the world: they knew where to go and how to do it. It was a great pleasure to work with Floris and he taught me the rudiments of the profession. In the morning, we arrived at the agency, the radio was permanently on, we picked up telexes from AFP, the Associated Press, Reuters… As the news gradually came in, we watched stories being born. In Bangladesh, for example. By midday, we already had the skeleton of a reportage mapped out. At four, Floris would say: "Sebastião, are you ready?" I would rush home, pack my bag and by eleven I was boarding a plane to Dhaka. In the meantime, Gamma had secured publication guarantees from various magazines, so I couldn't afford to fail.

Before leaving, Floris would hand me a press file and, thanks to my university studies, I was quickly able to analyze the situation and work out how to tackle the country. If I was working for *Paris Match*, *Time*, *Stern* or *Newsweek*, there might be a contact or organization already on the ground. In any case, when I arrived, I managed to meet other photographers and journalists. I contacted as many people as possible. At that time, everything was easier: the world was essentially divided into two blocks. In order to begin to comprehend a given situation, the first step consisted of placing it in a specific geopolitical logic between the Soviet Union and the United States, bearing in mind that the French always formed a small, separate block. Then I set to work. In the evening, I went to the airport, where I handed over my rolls of film to some passengers. I always found volunteers and never lost a film. I let Gamma know by telex, describing my photos and the passengers who were carrying them, in order to facilitate the task of our motorcyclist, who had to arrange to be at the door of the aircraft to pick them up. As soon as the photos reached Gamma, they were developed and, the same day, distributed to the magazines.

If anything happened somewhere else in the world, I went straight there from wherever I was at the time. From the Congo, for example, I dashed off to Sudan or to Egypt, before returning to Paris. For those who were fortunate enough to work there, Gamma was a true education. I owe much to Floris. In addition, as I have already said, my studies had provided me with excellent tools to tackle this job and the desire to explore things in depth. In the course of time, I got to know several countries well, to understand how certain mechanisms worked and to see the problems of our constantly changing world emerge.

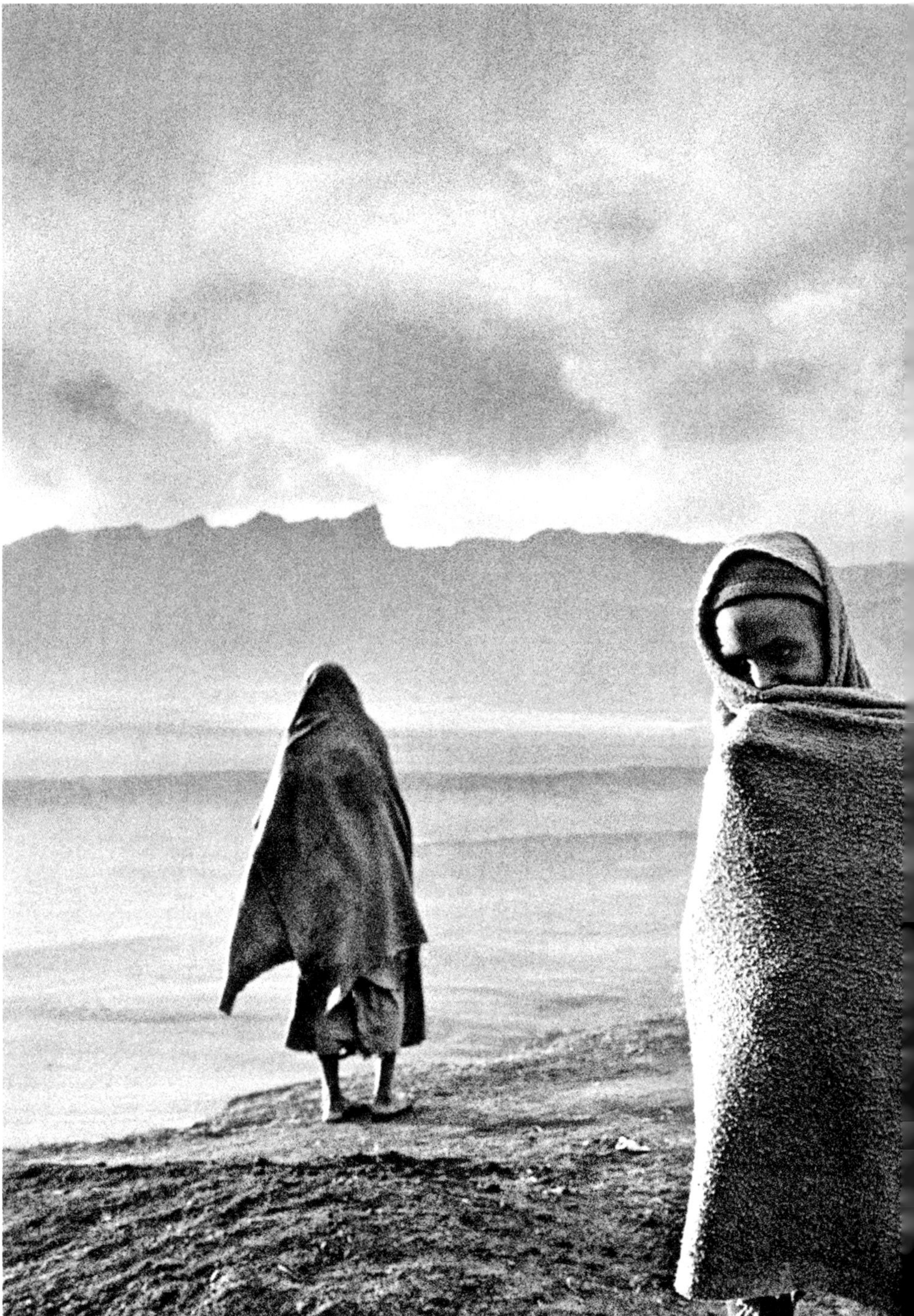

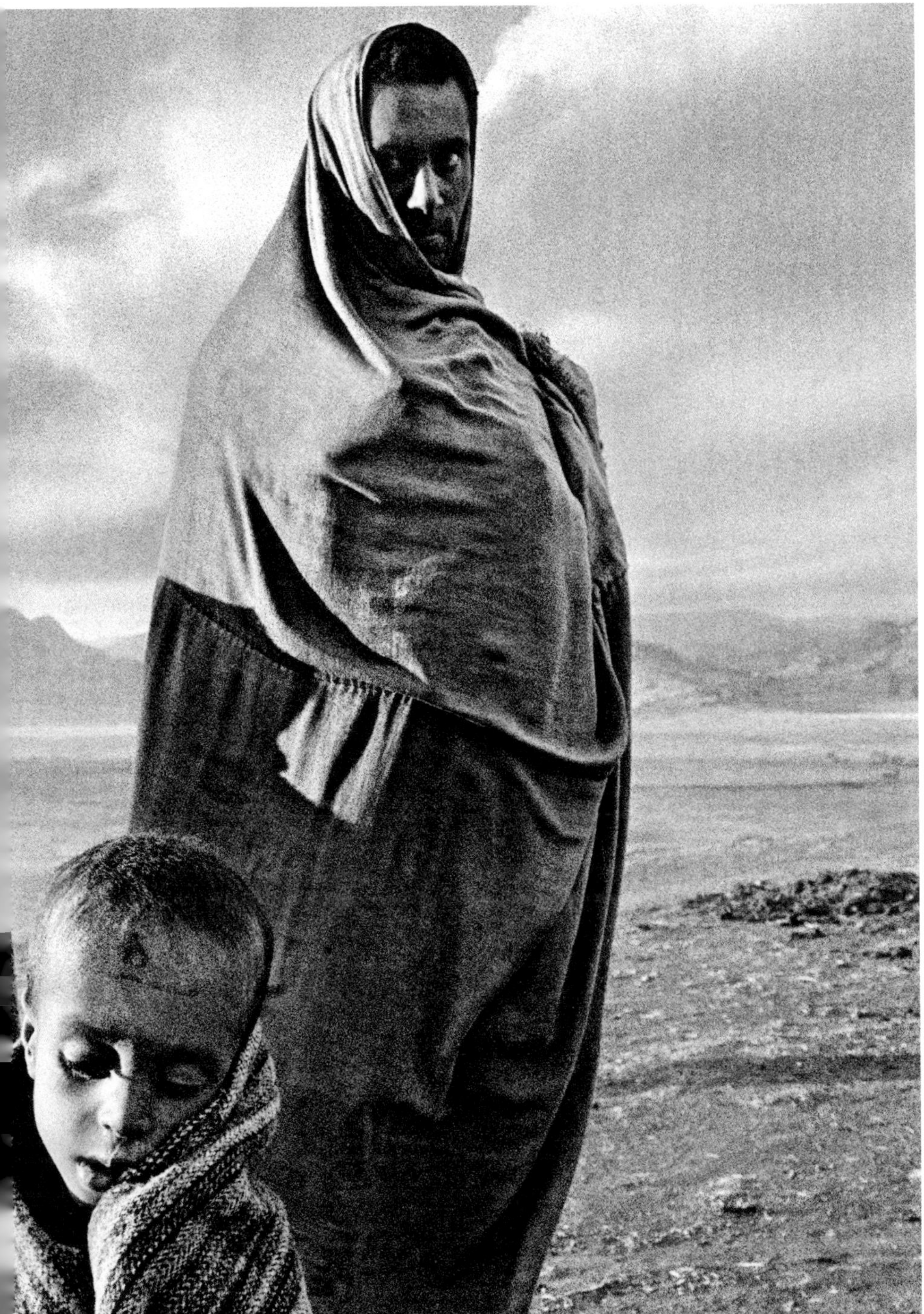

Refugees waiting outside Korem camp, Ethiopia, 1984

Photography, my way of life

Some think of me as a photojournalist. It isn't true. Others think I am an activist. That isn't true either. The only truth is that photography is my life. All my photos correspond to moments that I have experienced intensely. All these images exist because life, my life, has driven me to make them. Because there was an anger in me that led me to that particular place. Sometimes, I am guided by an ideology, sometimes simply by curiosity or by my desire to be there. My photography is not objective at all. Like all photographers, I take photographs depending on myself, what happens to be going through my head, what I'm thinking and experiencing. And I take it on.

All my photos have ended up in newspapers, sure. The press is my principal means of support, my point of reference. Nevertheless, for me, to photograph means much more than publishing images. For a magazine, you work for four or five days, a week at most, on the same subject, particularly nowadays. My work, however, is never finished. What interests me is to produce photographic essays subdivided into various reportages staggered over several years. To work on a theme in depth for five or six years, rather than flitting from one subject to another, from one place to another. The only way to tell a story is to return to the same place several times; with this dialectic, you develop it. I have continued like this for over forty years and it has given my work a certain coherence. This coherence is also certainly due to my emotional stability. To the fact of having spent my whole life with the woman I love; thanks to everything we have shared together and with our children. Now, when I look back, I discover a harmony in who I am, what I do and where I come from. But, of course, at the time, I knew only that I was living intensely.

In the beginning, Lélia and I didn't have much money and it wasn't easy. But I had no regrets about abandoning my career as an economist. Over the years, this hasn't changed, I still love photography deeply, framing a shot. In addition, photography has always allowed me to follow the tides of history. One day, perhaps it will be replaced by another language, but in the meantime, it offers moments of intensity to those who practice it, and a privileged life.

Photographers' closest cousins are architects, as I have discovered through Lélia's studies. Like us, they navigate between fullness and emptiness, issues of light, line and movement, in the quest for consistency between their way of life, their ideology, their history. In the end, all of this is related. That is the magic of architecture, like photography. Unlike cinema or television, photography has the power to produce images that are not continuous frames but fragments of frames. Fractions of a second that tell whole stories. In my images, the life of every person encountered is told through his eyes, his expressions and what he is doing.

To take good photos, you have to experience great pleasure. It is impossible to spend five years of your life in Africa, unless you truly love that continent. It is useless to force yourself to watch people working if you are not interested in it. To spend several months in a mine, you have to be extremely motivated. You have to love all of this. Anyone who lives with a photographer knows this: the most boring thing in the world is to follow one. He can spend many hours at a stretch in the same place, eyes fixed on his viewfinder. I love passing time like this, watching, composing a shot, working on the light in depth. Everything is then decided in the lab. I have to try to translate my emotions into a language that is not real, since black and white is an abstraction, realized through the range of greys of the photographic print. In the past, I experienced this pleasure on my own in the laboratory, but nowadays I entrust the silver printing to Dominique Granier.

Before I started to use a digital camera, when I set off to film long reportages, I often had to wait for several months before being able to develop the films that I was carrying rewound in metal containers. It was only when I returned to Paris that I was able to verify whether the magic I had felt on the spot had been recorded on film; whether I had succeeded, or not, in capturing those images I had waited for so long, spending days with a particular community, participating in its life, taking part in its activities, watching, almost spying at times, crouching somewhere for hours on end.

Totally integrated with his surroundings, the photographer knows that he is going to witness something unexpected. When he merges into the landscape, into that particular situation, the construction of the image eventually emerges before his eyes. But in order to see it, he has to be part of what is happening. Then, all the elements will start to play in his favour. Those moments are wonderful! It reminds me of the work I carried out for a book commissioned by the Comité d'Entreprise de la SNCF, the French national railway company: I was in the station at Aurillac, in the Massif Central, where twenty or so people were at work. I was with Antoine de Giaglis, a friend from the CGT, who suddenly said to me: "Look, Sebastião, the whole station is working with your camera". It was true. Everyone was going about his own business, but it was as though we were all connected and part of a great theatrical drama on the same stage. We were all busy performing the same play, together. That's what photography is. At a certain moment, all the elements are connected: the people, the wind, the trees, the background, the light.

When I take a shot, I am completely absorbed in my action. It is magical and a personal pleasure. Now that I am growing older, I need an assistant, a travel companion. But for a long time, I did everything on my own—in Latin America, for example, where I lived for months in the mountains, with the Indians.

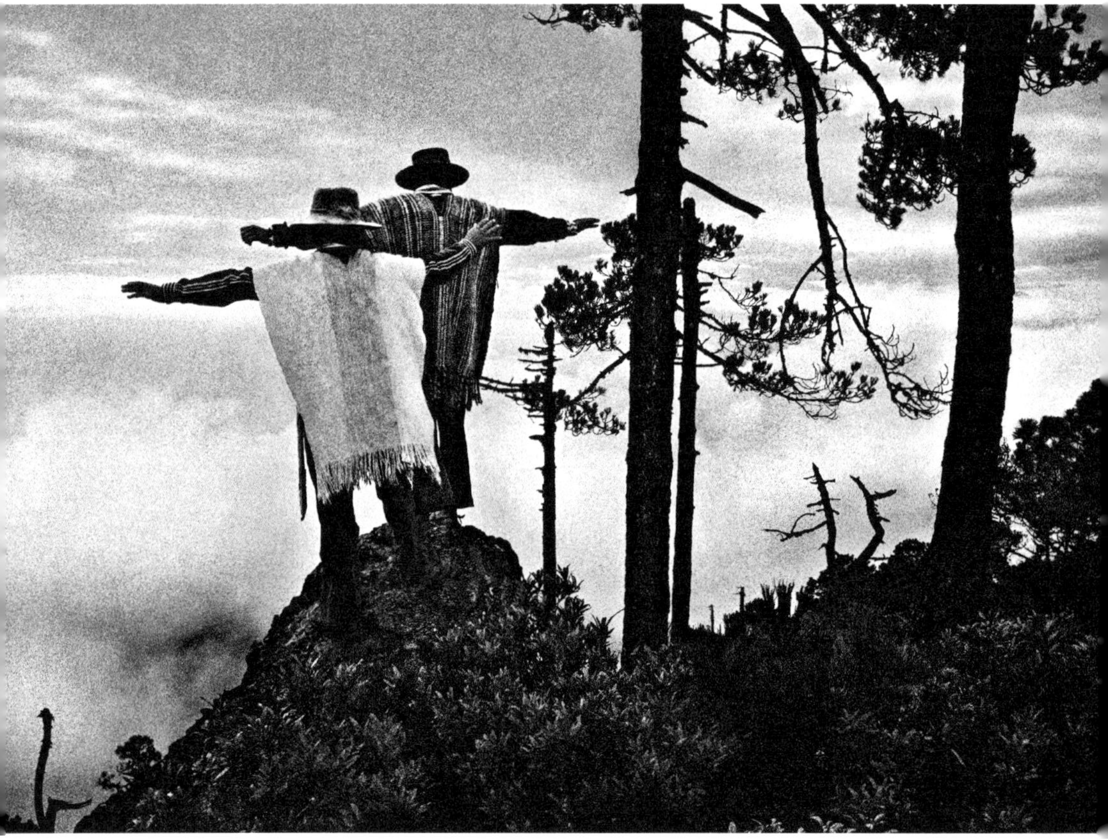

Prayer to the Mixe God Kioga, Mexico, 1980

Other Americas

Like Africa, South America occupies an important place in my life as a photographer, and in my life as a whole. At Gamma, whenever I began to speak about it, no one was interested. Nevertheless, it was essential for me to go there. I really wanted to photograph those countries, it was a way for me to get closer to my own culture. These countries are different to Brazil, but I needed to experience that other America. Ever since I was a child, I had always heard talk of the mountains of Chile, Bolivia, Peru. They were part of my imaginary world. I absolutely had to go there, to live there. And so I went, returning there often between 1977 and 1984. I also visited Ecuador, Guatemala and Mexico. In 1979, thanks to an amnesty, I was able to return to Brazil and so I began to photograph my own country. I loved working in the different communities of Indians, with their workers in the cities or the countryside, with the mountain communities and the indigenous minorities. I discovered the mysticism of the Sertão, the Northeast of Brazil, with its men dressed in leather and their struggle for survival in this semi-arid land. I also travelled across the Sierra Madre, the chain of Mexican mountains that merges into the mist... This task lasted seven years, sometimes I say seven centuries, and allowed me to travel through cultures in which time unfolds to the rhythm of the past.

It always took several months to approach the various Indian populations. To set my project up, prepare my reportages and make contact with the organizations that would put me in touch with the indigenous minorities. Then, I had to manage to reach those communities. After the plane, I caught the bus, like the Indians. Finally, I had to go on foot. Each time, it would take me several days to find this group or that in the mountains. Once I reached my destination, I had to wait until they accepted me, even though I had obtained authorization in advance. These Indios, these peoples of enormous culture, have in large part been massacred by our Western civilization. They are still mistrustful. You have to talk with them at length, live with them, if you then want to photograph them.

I was often away from home for months and I missed my wife terribly. I often thought of her and of Juliano, our little son. How many times did I go into a corner to cry! At the same time, however, I experienced enormous pleasure in seeking out these photos. On the other hand, it was impossible to travel so far, make such an expensive journey and stay in the place for just a few days. I learnt a lot in those high mountains. I suffered from the cold, it's freezing at night, and it was years before I bought myself a good sleeping bag. But I saw so much beauty and discovered so much cultural and spiritual richness, that I don't have any regrets.

I did not realize the images I took there alone. It was necessary for the people to allow me to do so, that they should offer them to me. And they did so only because I took the time to live with them. The fact that I had gone alone also proved essential. The human being is a sociable animal and when he arrives somewhere alone, he immediately allows himself to be taken in by those who live there. When I was cold, when I was hungry, when I was missing my family, I told my hosts. I spoke to them about my small son who was growing up far away from me. In other words, I shared the most important things with them, just as they shared these images with me. It was they who gave me these photos, and I received them. To me, they are filled with a real power. When I look at them, they evoke my isolation, but also the comfort these Indians were able to provide for me. When I have shown them, they

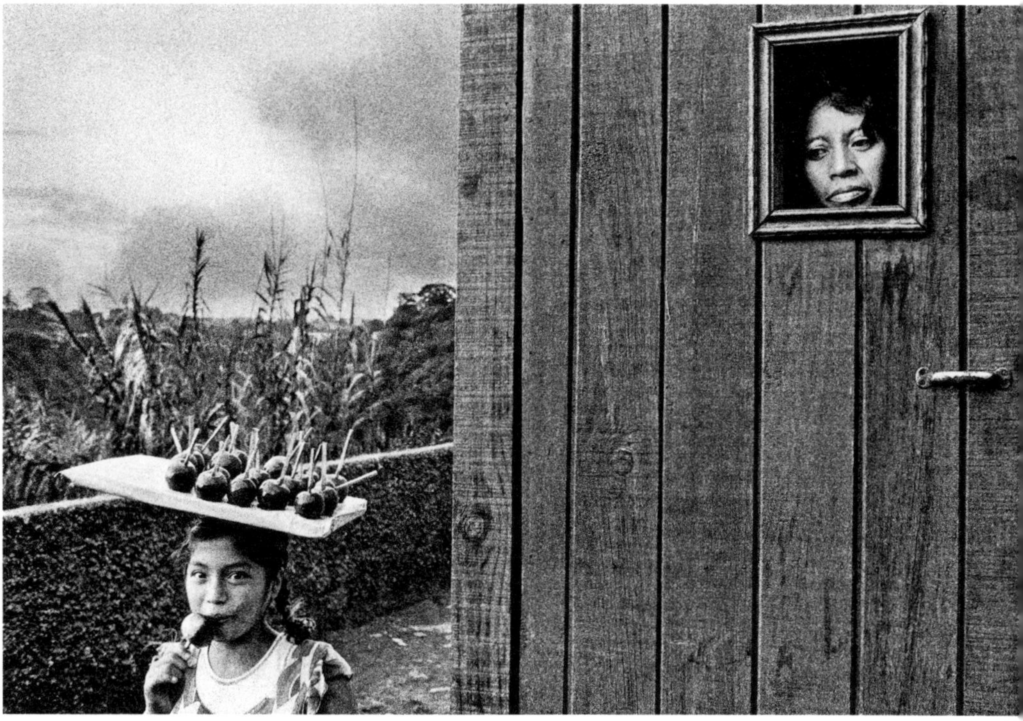

Guatemala, 1978

have sometimes transmitted this power, reflecting the life of these people and the times we spent together.

On my return, this project, in which nobody had been interested beforehand, received a Prix de la Ville de Paris, for a first photographic book. I was thus able to publish *Autres Ameriques* (Other Americas) with Claude Nori, at the publishing house Éditions Contrejour. Claude, who is also a photographer himself, is a fantastic editor: he has created wonderful books with Doisneau, Willy Ronis, Jeanloup Sieff… The Prix de la Ville de Paris allowed forty-nine photos to be published, plus one on the cover. It was the first book that Lélia had designed and produced. Our first book. In 1986, we staged an exhibition in Paris, at the Maison de l'Amérique Latine. This exhibition then travelled the world.

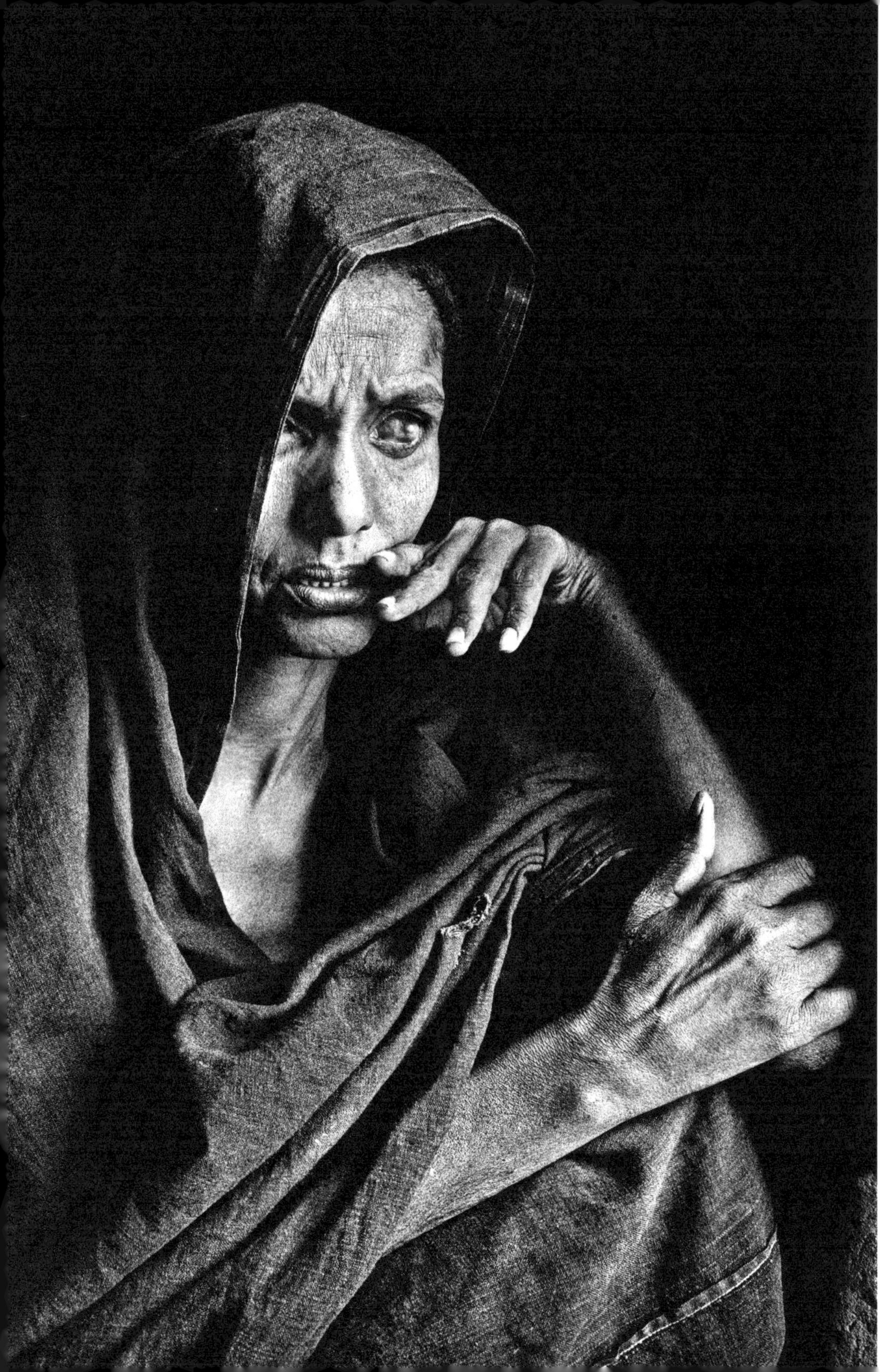

Images of a world in distress

In 1984, Médicins sans Frontières (Doctors without Borders) launched a major campaign to provide food and medical aid to the populations affected by the drought that was devastating the Sahel and leaving its people starving. With this organization, over eighteen months I carried out a major reportage in Mali, Ethiopia, Chad and Sudan; a series of images showing armies of refugees fleeing from hunger, thirst and, in some cases, war. Hoards of uprooted people were seen streaming towards camps, such as Korem, in Ethiopia, the largest at the time, where up to 80,000 victims had gathered. My photos appeared in the international press. The French daily newspaper *Libération* followed this reportage closely, I was working directly with Christian Caujolle, who was its picture editor at the time. This series of publications made a huge contribution to the humanitarian cause. In 1985, I received the World Press Photo Award and the Oskar Barnack Prize for this work. The following year, in France, Robert Delpire conceived a book published by the Centre National de la Photographie entitled *Sahel, l'homme en détresse*. In 1988, Lélia produced a second book to mark the opening of Médicins sans Frontières' branch in Spain, entitled *Sahel, el fine del camino.*

In the course of my life, I have carried out numerous reportages on refugees and struggling populations. As in all my photographic essays, each time I have introduced myself to the people and communities through the institutions and organizations who are working with them. I have taken the time to meet people and to talk to them. I always face those

Refugee waiting for the distribution of food, Gundam, Mali, 1985

I am photographing in their environment, in their actions. I never ask anyone to pose, but they know perfectly well that I am taking their photo and they tacitly agree. No photo, on its own, can change poverty in the world. Nevertheless, combined with text, films and all the efforts of humanitarian and environmental organizations, my images are part of a wider movement denouncing violence, exclusion and ecological issues. These means of information contribute to raising awareness in those who see them, of the ability of all of us to change the destiny of humanity.

I do not originate from the North of the planet and I don't share the same feelings of guilt as some of my colleagues do. I don't photograph material poverty because I feel guilty, it is part of the world I come from. Since the left has taken the reins, and at Lula's instigation in particular, Brazil has started to develop. When I was young, it was an under-developed country and, before I left, I had seen poverty increase. I have always found unjust the way in which wealth is redistributed between North and South. I wanted to show the famine in Africa to the inhabitants of the wealthy countries so that they might be aware that it is the primary consequence of a global imbalance. For the same reason, I wanted the voice of the landless in Brazil to be heard.

In 1979, when I was able to return to Brazil, I was struck by the poverty. During the dictatorship, from 1964 to 1984, a large portion of Brazil's small rural landowners had sold their land for an "attractive price" to large farming enterprises and had been hit by the hyperinflation of that time. It was as though they had been dispossessed and, since then, they had led a precarious existence. The first photos that I

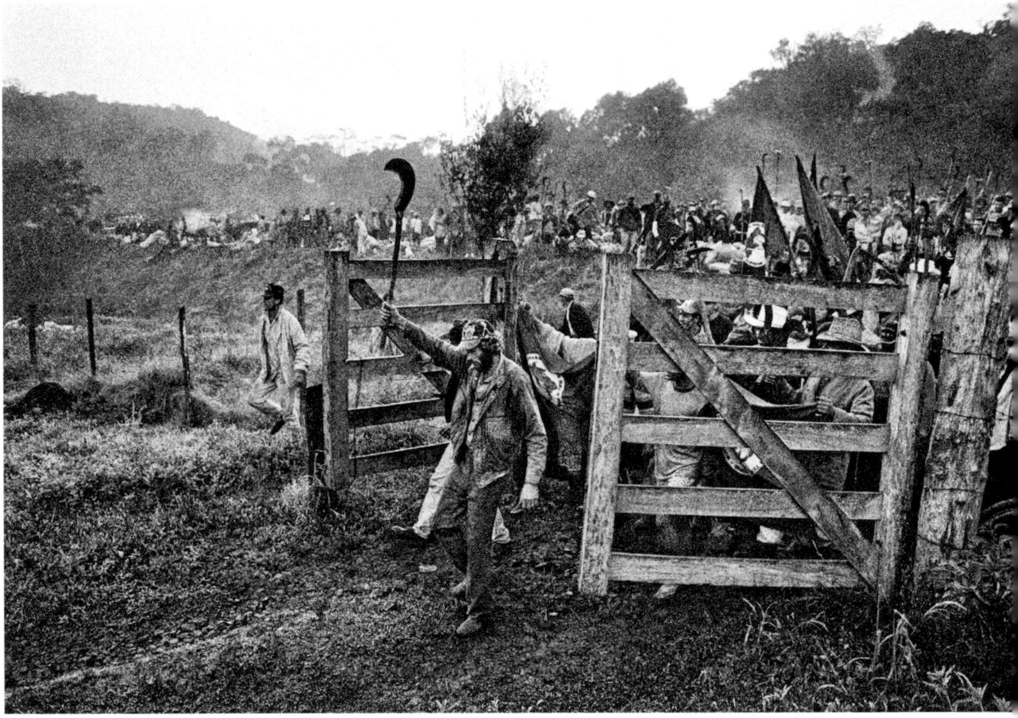

State of Paraná, Brazil, 1996

took, on my return, showed the situation of these farmers, known as *boias frias* (those who eat cold food). They were living on the fringes of immense agricultural estates created by grouping together their land. For a long time, on the spot, it was only the Church of the Liberation Theology that had reacted. The grassroot communities, as well as FETAG (The Federation of Agricultural Workers), provided these disinherited people with the opportunity to meet and to raise a voice of protest against this injustice.

In 1984, the Movimento dos Trabalhadores Sem Terra (Landless Worker's Movement), known as the MST, was formed, involving 4.8 million rural families. For fifteen years or so, I followed its demands. The MST has conducted a census of all the uncultivated land in the country. By occupying it, it wanted to force the government to reacquire this land in order to redistribute it to the dispossessed workers. So, in 1996, in Paranà, a state in the south of Brazil, I watched 12,000 people, roughly 3,200 families, occupy a property of 83,000 hectares, only 12,000 of which were cultivated.

The MST acted legally and harmed no one, as it only occupied uncultivated land. The Brazilian constitution stipulates that it is forbidden to own land if it is not used. This did not prevent the great property owners from breaking the law: many of them had drawn on the services of their henchmen or the police to have the families who were occupying their land expelled. Thanks to the MST, however, much of this land was eventually redistributed at the time to about 200,000 families. After roughly fifteen years, I realized that my images told this story. So Lélia produced a book with an introduction by José Saramago, the poems of Brazilian composer and singer Chico Buarque and my images. Published in 1996, *Terra* constituted a true manifesto for the MST, written by four-hands. Lélia also conceived the most original of exhibitions, in the form of two thousand kits of fifty posters, easy to install. The aim was to raise funds, but also to publicize the story of these fighters for the land. These selling exhibitions were organized in Latin America, the United States, Europe and Asia. All the profits went to the MST. In France, Italy and Spain, we set up travelling exhibitions with the organization Frères des Hommes.

Each of my photos is a choice. Even in difficult situations, you have to want to be there and to assume the responsibility for being there. Adhering or not to what is happening, but always knowing why you are in a certain place. Following the landless was my way of participating in their movement. Showing images of famine in Africa, a way of denouncing it. Everywhere, these images have provoked reaction. Photography is a language that is all the more powerful because it can be read anywhere in the world without the need for translation.

From Magnum to Amazonas Images

Jean Gaumy, one of my colleagues at Gamma, joined the Magnum photo agency in 1977. A year later, Raymond Depardon followed him. I was very happy at Gamma where, with Hervé Tardy, I had created a magazine section in which we did some excellent work. Nevertheless, in 1979, I presented my portfolio to Magnum, and they accepted me. At the time, Lélia was expecting our second child, Rodrigo.

When he was born, a few days after I started at Magnum, we discovered that he had Down's syndrome. With Rodrigo, we were thrown into the world of disability, about which we knew nothing. A world we had to discover and tame. It is one of the greatest and most painful adventures in our life. It has also taught us a lot. I have laughed so much with Rodrigo, he was adorable and so funny when he was small. He is an endless source of sweetness and affection. I am sure that without him, my photos would have been different. He has led me to look at faces differently, to approach individuals in another way.

Gamma had been my great school of photography, but Magnum offered me a formidable opportunity to grow. As for Lélia, once she had finished her master's degree in urban planning, she developed the Magnum Gallery, organizing exhibitions that enabled her to gain valuable experience. My first assignment for the agency came from the German magazine *Geo*: a reportage in Guyana. They wanted me to take the images in colour. I am known for my love of black and white, but from the start of my career up until the beginning of my series entitled *Workers*, I often worked in colour. My final reportage in colour, an assignment for *Life* in 1987, celebrated the seventieth anniversary of the Russian revolution. I had proposed a reportage in black and white, and the editorial team had agreed. Jimmy Fox, Magnum's editor in chief, had asked me to take some images in colour for the agency's archives. So, from Moscow I sent all my films straight to *Life* in New York, black and white, as well as colour. The magazine developed them all and, forgetting my initial proposal, published several double page spreads in colour of parades and fireworks in the Red Square. These were my last photos in colour to be published.

I remained at Magnum for fifteen years. It was stimulating, but also highly competitive. I met some great photographers, including Erich Hartmann, Henri Cartier-Bresson, Eric Lessing and George Rodger, who became great friends. It was a great pleasure to mix with these strong personalities, but I also witnessed some terrible arguments.

When I arrived at the agency, I had already had a relationship with all the big magazines. So, in March 1981, the *New York Times* commissioned a reportage from me on the first hundred days of Ronald Reagan's presidency—he had been elected in November of the previous year. On the 30th of March, in Washington, in broad daylight, the president of the United States was shot as he came out of his hotel. I was there, and I began to take pictures. I witnessed the six gunshots fired by a deranged person at the presidential staff. Reagan wasn't directly hit, but a bullet that ricocheted off his car subsequently lodged in his chest and was extracted several hours later in the operating theatre. This attempt on Reagan's life was terrible for him, but very interesting for me and for Magnum, which was in financial difficulty at the time:

all my photos were sold! Later that same day, at the entrance to the White House, I met a photographer who had been present when Bob Kennedy was assassinated. That's how he introduced himself, it was even written on his business card. I sensed the danger: I had been photographing Africa for years, I was working in depth on Latin America at the time, however I risked being classified as the photographer of the assassination attempt on Reagan. So Lélia and I decided that we would never allow these images to be published again. Nevertheless, I confess that it was a great "coup", and it largely contributed to financing my reportages, my own personal work, not on assignment, in other words, everything that was truly close to my heart.

Many photographers worked for Magnum, each with a different way of conducting their profession. At the dawn of the twenty-first century, the world in which the agency had been created, back in 1948, and the press of that time no longer existed: they had had to evolve. I was not the only one carrying out reportages that did not follow the news stories of the moment, but showed the changes taking place in the world. Others doing the same were Gilles Peress, Abbas, James Nachtwey... Our method of working barely resembled that of our colleagues who were working in colour for the geographical magazines, or of those who worked in advertising or reported the events of the year. It was necessary to consider a division into different sections in order to respond to the specific needs of all the photographers, enabling them to manage their archives better and to sell their images more successfully. So, I proposed that Magnum set up a series of production units. I was sure that this would lead to greater profitability and consistency, but my idea was not accepted. It took me two years to decide, before I finally left the agency.

At the time of my departure, I had already published several books and many museums around the world had exhibited my photos. I had stipulated contracts with *Paris Match*, *Life*, *Stern*, *El País*, to launch a new project entitled *Migrations*. I needed to have a team to support me. Magnum refused to create this, so Lélia and I came up with it on our own.

As far as the marketing of the images was concerned, we searched for agents in various countries around the world. Selling has never been our trade, but we knew how to create projects that tell stories, how to plan and realize reportages. Lélia was experienced in organizing exhibitions, at every stage from conception through to installation, and she had already produced several books. The time was ripe and she was ready to launch and direct our own organization. So, in 1994, we established Amazonas Images[1], our own agency, situated on the banks of the Canal Saint-Martin in Paris. We recruited a handful of employees; documentary film-makers, analogic print specialists and, late on, digital print specialists. Otherwise, we sub-contracted certain jobs to outside laboratories.

1. www.amazonasimages.com

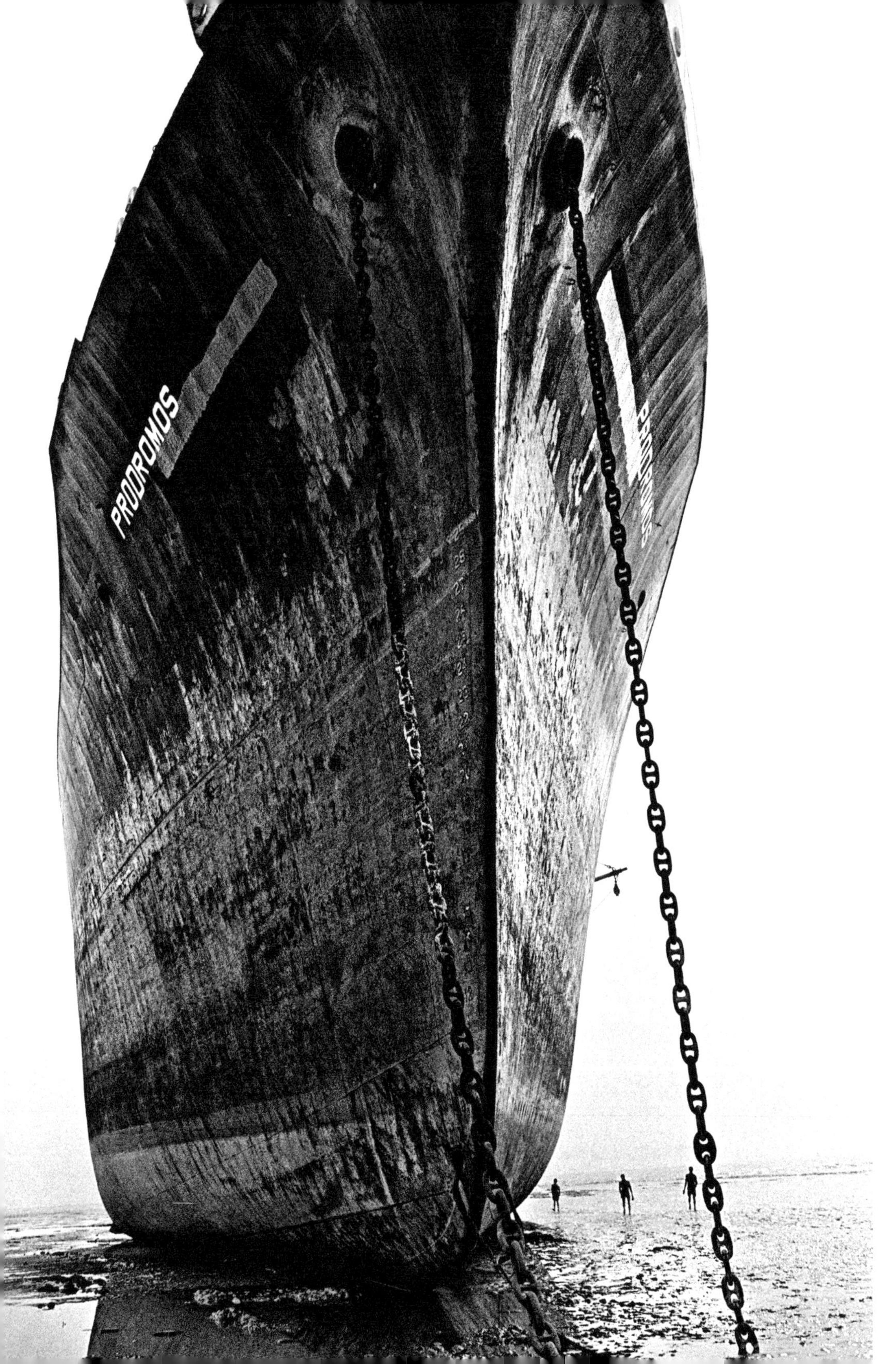
PRODROMOS

Workers

In the mid-1980s, when Lélia and I conceived the project entitled (in English) *Workers*, we wanted to pay tribute to labour. In order to explain this better, I shall return to economics. Every product is the result of the combination of raw material, capital and labour. Taking this analysis further, we realize that, of the three factors, labour is the most important. Let's consider, for example, the Amazonian Indians, whose life resembles our own five or ten thousand years ago. They know how to smoke fish—the smoking of the fish sold in supermarkets on a more or less industrial scale derives from this ancestral experience. Technology has allowed the mechanization of manual labour without which it would not exist. As for money, it makes the human labour become the property of capital. It is undeniable that the most important component in production is labour. I conceived a series of reportages intended to pay tribute to labour and workers. During the five years I devoted to it, no one refused to be photographed while working, and I was able to show a world of production in action. A world that is disappearing.

I focused on large scale production, where man was still important. We were experiencing the end of the great industrial revolution. Technological advancement, the discovery of electronics and then robotics, had begun to replace the human hand. For example, in the automobile industry, for a long time every component on a production line was handled by workers. Men or women bolted the various pieces together. Then robots appeared to replace the human arms. Before it was swept away, I wanted to establish a visual archaeology of

Chittagong, Bangladesh, 1989

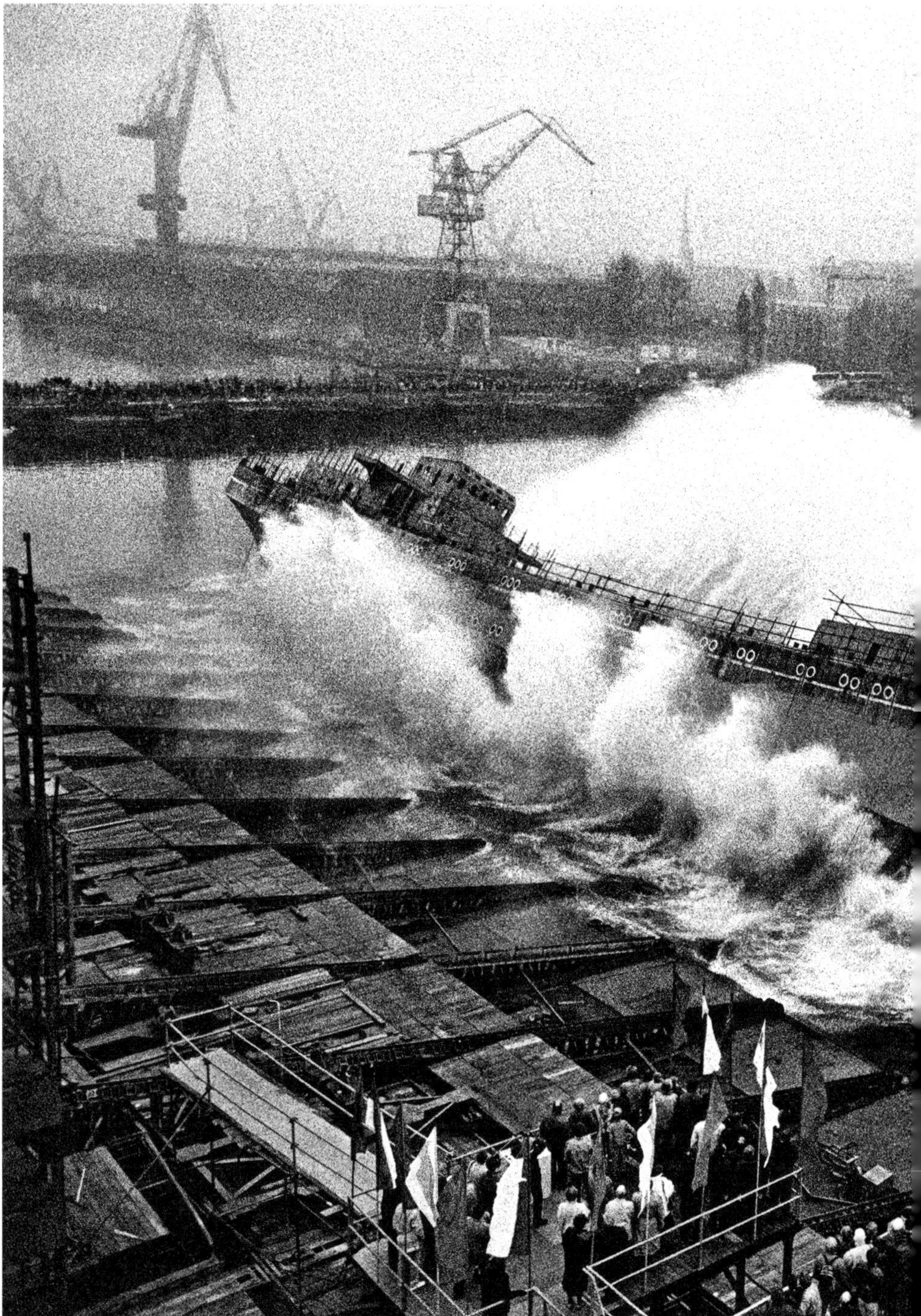

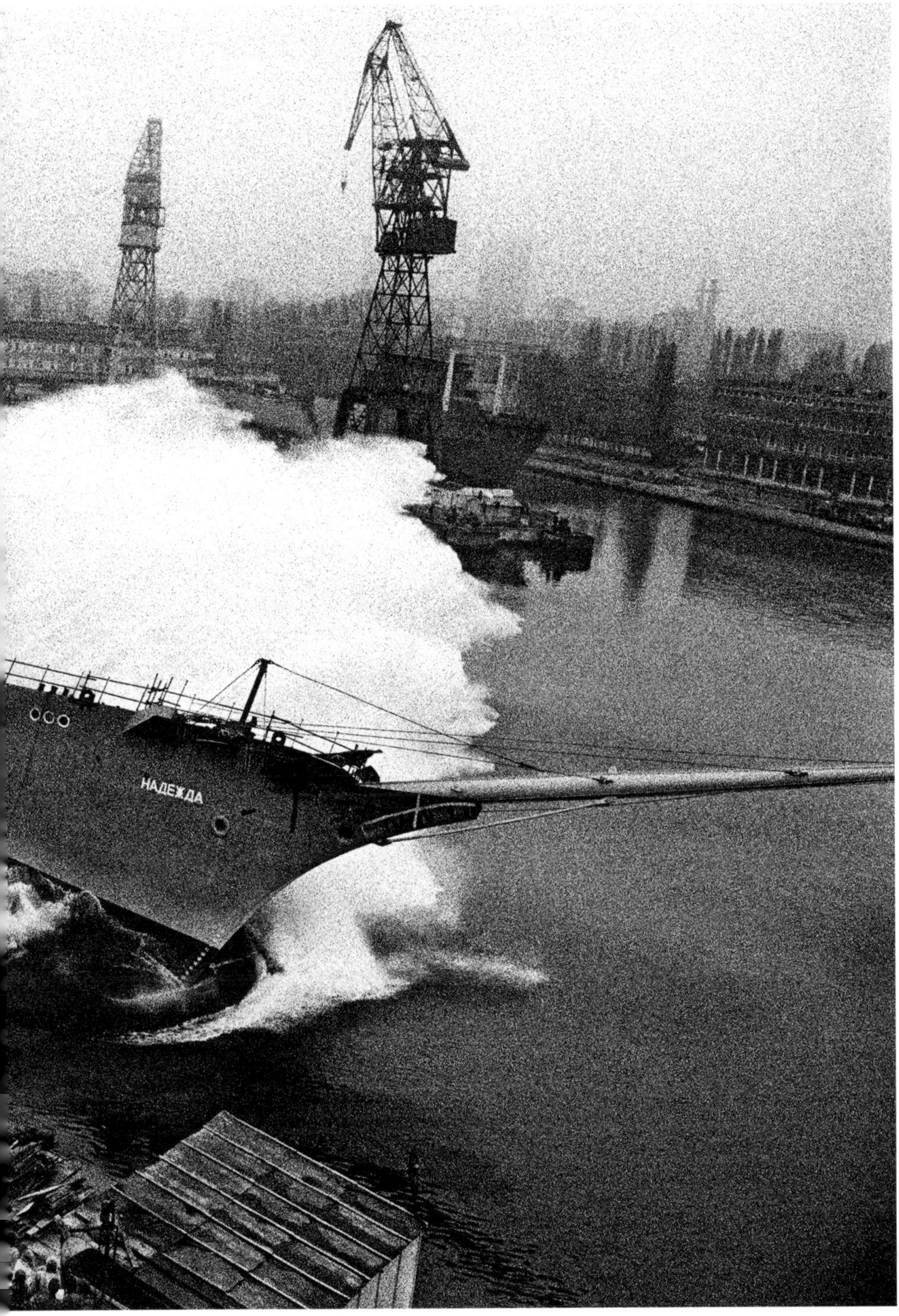

Naval shipyards, Danzig, Poland, 1990

the industrial era. To do this, I visited industrial agricultural plantations, factories and mines. I went to where one can best see labour applied to raw material, where one can observe work on the production line.

Between 1986 and 1991, with the support of a group of editors in chief—including Roger Thérond of *Paris Match* and Alberto Anaut of *El País*—and of Magnum, the agency I still worked for at the time, I realized about forty reportages in twenty-five countries. Very few in Europe, since, during the 1980s, many industries were starting to be delocalized, as turnkeys, in China, Brazil, Indonesia and India. Entire industries, such as metal-working in Lorraine, thus disappeared from our landscape. I loved this period in my life because wherever I found man working, he was proud to be producing, creating. I was impressed by the ingenuity of the human race, capable of taking a piece of steel, welding it to another, then another... and, little by little, of making for example a ship out of it. A great monument, of remarkable sophistication. Before it is put in water, it is a heap of assembled scrap-metal. But as soon as it touches the water, it becomes a ship, and once it is fitted out, it sails away... It is incredible that a scrap of metal can float... And all of this, originally, goes back to the invention of the first dugout canoe that man was capable of keeping afloat. The technique is the same, as is the initial achievement. This ship carries products of all kinds, or passengers, it connects the various parts of the world. When it is judged to be too old, the ship is taken to Bangladesh, to certain parts of India or Pakistan where little metal is available. It is broken up and becomes a multitude of pieces of metal again. These are transformed into knives, agricultural tools and other objects identical to those the ship transported, across the seas, in the course of its life.

The bronze propellers become teapots, earrings, decorations on the clothing of the women of Bengal, adorned with magnificent jewellery. Beforehand, they have sailed around the world, visited the harbours of Singapore, New York and the rest of the planet. This process is very sophisticated, incredibly complex. Observing it, I was amazed at how incredible the human race is. But there is also the other side of the coin. A ship is born in coal and iron mines: coal and iron make steel, which is transformed in its turn into the sheets that make up the ship. The silicosis that eats away at the lungs of the coal and iron miners affects the shipyard workers in the same way. The same symptoms are found in Bangladesh, in the ship breaking yards. This disease runs through the whole industrial chain. Thanks to *Workers*, I was able to witness this geopolitics of production.

I have noticed that sometimes, at the very moment that life is created, death is also being prepared. In Kazakhstan, the same industries produce phosphate, used as a fertilizer, and napalm, an extremely efficient weapon in war. In Bangladesh, using the same ancestral methods of weaving, they make sacks for grain and those that, when filled with sand, serve to fortify trenches and protect soldiers: under the impact of bullets, the jute sacks close up without spilling their sand and remain an effective protection barrier. Sugar plantations in Brazil also have a diversified production; from the cane, one can obtain either sugar or methanol, a fuel that pollutes much less than petrol. In Cuba, visiting the sugar plantations, I realized that it was not man who made the cane, but the cane that made man. Whether they are in Brazil or Cuba, the workers on these plantations are as alike as two drops of water: they are identical in the way they work, move, dress and even enjoy themselves.

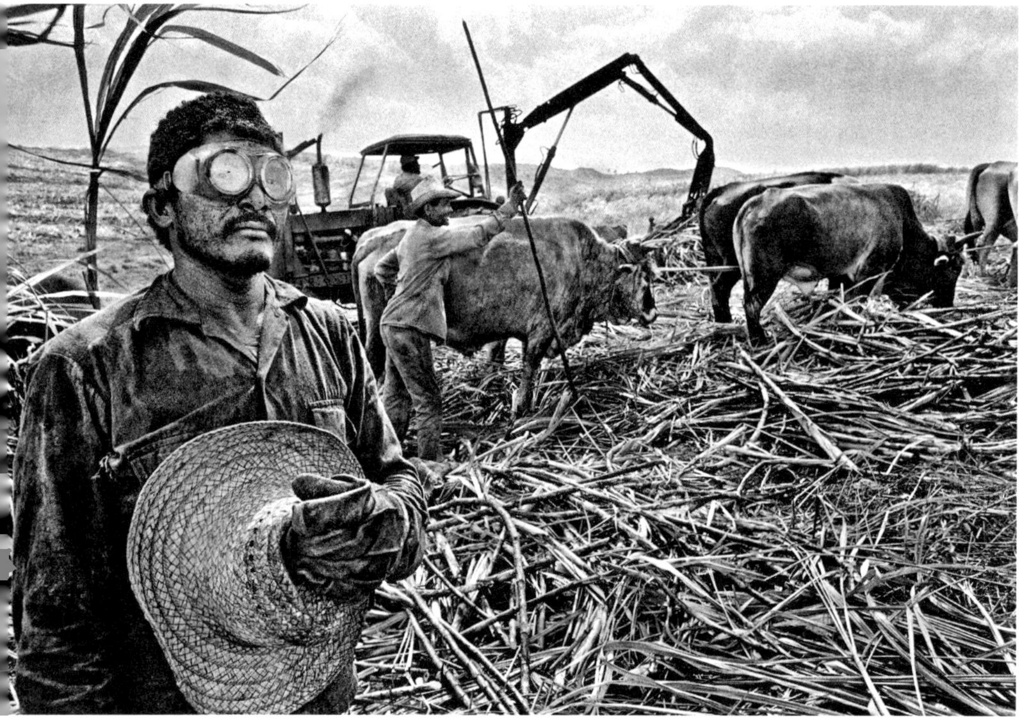

Sugarcane harvesters, Havana, Cuba, 1988

Also in Cuba, just a few kilometres from the sugar plantations, I met tobacco pickers—they belonged to a completely different universe. They wore caps on their heads to approach the tobacco leaves destined to become famous vintage cigars, like the great vintages of the prestigious vineyards in France. These workers were nothing like the sugar cane cutters, yet they were neighbours; they bore much more resemblance to workers involved in winegrowing. I realized that it is the product that makes the man. The delicate nature of working with the tobacco called for special measures. During the rolling process, for example, somebody told stories. In the past, they chose tales like the legend of King Arthur. While I was there, I happened to listen to the life of Lenin, of Marx and other tales of political revolutions. Whatever the case, it was

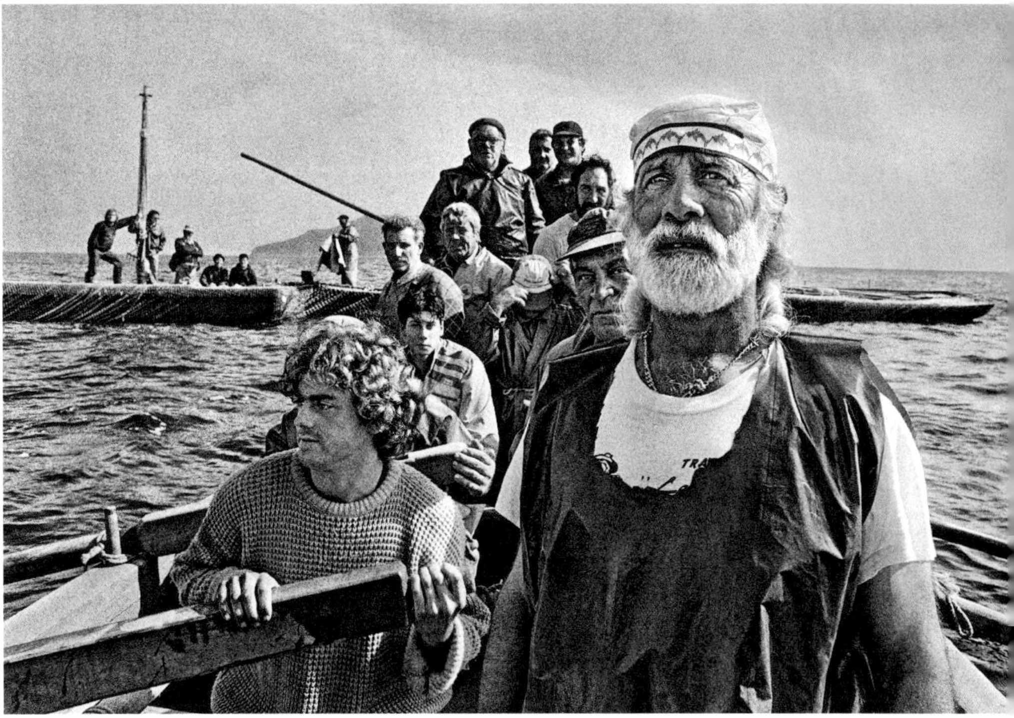

Mattanza, traditional tuna fishing, Trapani, Italy, 1991

a matter of helping the workers to concentrate so that the results were perfect. It was an amazing method of production to watch!

I spent forty days on Réunion, the island of fragrances. I learnt how vetiver and geranium essences are produced, how vanilla is packed. I went off every morning with the *petits paysans du haut* (the inhabitants of the high part of the island) and I came back with them in the evening. I lived in the place, in the villages, and I had rented a room in the home of one of the inhabitants. Everywhere, in all the villages and all the various types of activity, I took my time. I spent many days with the tuna fishermen in Sicily, or observing the activity of the sea harvesters in Galicia, secretly watching women working with their faces entirely covered on the canal in Rajasthan, or following the workers in a hellish oilfield in Kuwait. I spent hours talking with some and with others, trying to understand them. After a while, they became used to me and in the end, I was almost part of the decor.

While working on these reportages, whatever the type of activity, I always chose to go into the great industries. It was relatively easy to gain access, and my aim was to relate the demise of an industrial world that had employed a huge number of people. Consequently, in 1989 I also went to China, to visit great units of production. It was the period of the repression of the protests in Tienanmen Square in Beijing. However, I had already been there before, and so they knew me. I never found any difficulty in photographing in this country, probably because I am Brazilian: Brazil has never posed a threat to the Chinese, because it was never part of the Cold War logic. I was always granted permits without difficulty, just as in the Soviet Union. I only had to be prepared well in advance and enter into the logic of the system. To wait until my application travelled through a bureaucracy in which no one dared to exercise his right to veto if the colleague before him had failed to use it.

This series of reportages took me to an abattoir in Dakota, the southern United States, where a thousand pigs were killed an hour, and two thousand cattle a day. The workers unremittingly repeated the same bloody gesture, in rooms without windows. The smell was appalling. The first day, it was impossible to take any photos, I was vomiting the whole time. The sight of this industrial sausage production put me off hot dogs forever. The staff was quite well paid, but it was one of the hardest jobs on a production line that I have ever seen.

On Java, in a little paradise of beauty, I watched men cover fifty kilometres on foot, there and back, across rice paddies, clove-growing plantations and the tropical jungle, before climbing to an altitude of 2,300 metres, then descending another 600 metres on the other side, and going down into the crater of the Kawah Ijen volcano, a great producer of sulphur. Due to the toxic emissions, veritable clouds of poison, it was necessary to breathe entirely through the mouth and not the nose. As their sole defence, the workers stuffed a piece of material into their mouth; in the course of time, their teeth were completely ruined. Even though none of them weighed more than 60 kilos, each filled a basket with 70 to 75 kilos of minerals. They fixed two baskets at either end of bamboo cane and then climbed the 600 metres separating them from the exit to the crater. This took them about two hours, then they hurtled down the slopes of the volcano, to avoid being crushed by the weight of the baskets. It was extremely dangerous. Some of them dislocated their kneecaps. At the time, they received about $3.50 per journey. Afterwards, they rested for a couple of days in order to recover physically, so that by the end of the month, they pocketed just enough to survive. I have equally strong memories of the time I spent in the gold and coal mines.

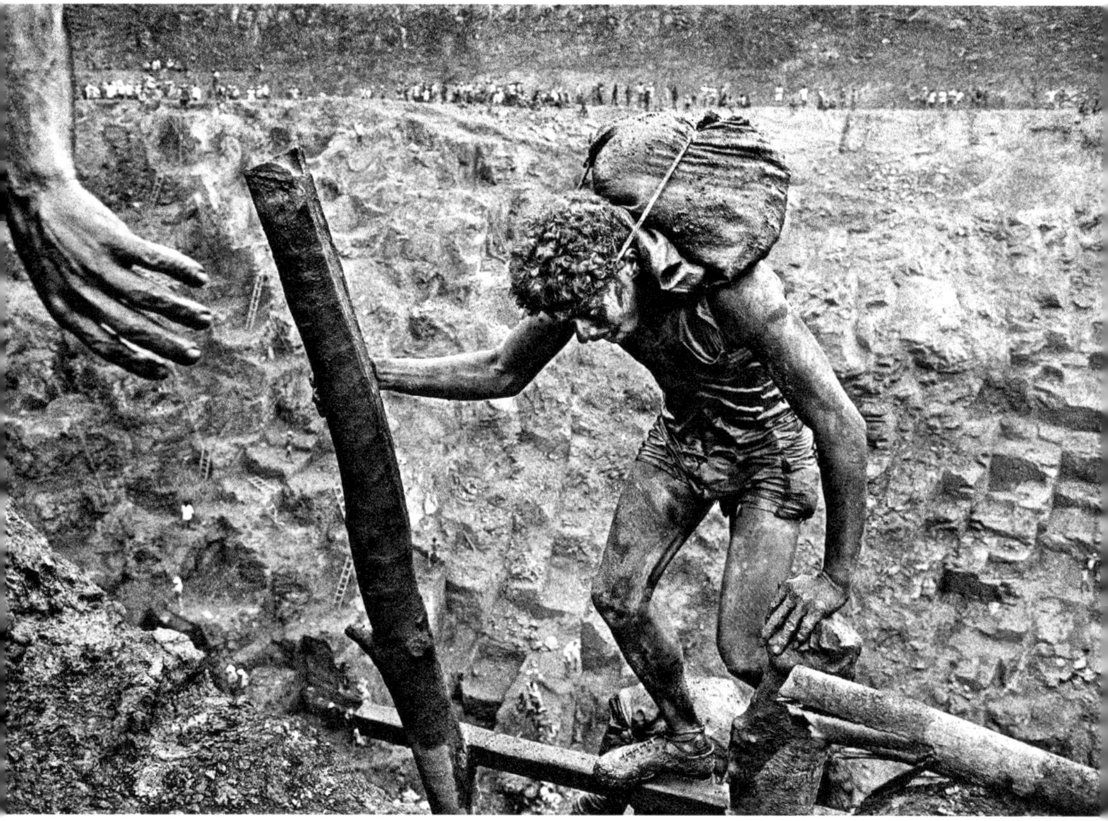

Open-air gold mine, Serra Pelada, State of Pará, Brazil, 1986

The world of the mines

The Serra Pelada gold mine, in the northern Brazilian state of Parà, was discovered in 1980, precipitating a gold rush. I wanted to see this, but the mine was managed by the federal police, and I was forbidden access on account of my record with the SNI (National Information Service) as a political protester. In 1986, when the management of the mine passed to the Miners' Co-operative, I finally obtained permission to go there. I was introduced by an old friend of my father, one of the thousands of owners. This enormous mine was divided into two or three thousand claims, each measuring 2 metres by 3, and employing fifteen to twenty people: payroll, guards, carriers, and so on. By the timc I went there, seventy thousand kilos of gold had already been extracted.

On the day I arrived, a miner asked me where I came from. I replied: "From Rio Doce", as that is the name of the valley where I was born. Without me realizing it, word quickly spread around the mine that I had been sent by the Vale do Rio Doce company, who were the legal owners of the concession. This company (now known as Vale) did in fact take its name from the valley where I was born and where it owns the largest iron mines in the world. At that time, it was starting to exploit the iron deposits in the state of Parà, where we found ourselves at that very moment. While, unbeknown to me, the rumour continued to spread, I discovered at my feet a hole as large as a football stadium. About fifty thousand men were working together, at a depth of around seventy metres, without a single mechanized tool.

They looked as though they were sculpted in the mud. Seeing all those people hammering with their pickaxes, digging the earth with their hands, I thought I heard the murmuring of the gold.

Suddenly, the noise stopped. All eyes were turned on me. With my pale skin and my light-coloured clothes—I always wear khaki when I work—I stood out among those thousands of sunburnt faces and those bodies splattered with ochre. Then they all began to bang their tools together, creating a deafening noise. I did not understand, so I took my cameras and started to photograph. Gradually, work began again.

I started to descend into the mine. Before reaching the bottom, I was entirely covered in mud, from my clothes to the straps of my camera, after being jostled by everyone I encountered. I could feel the tension in the air, and much hostility towards me. No one spoke to me, I couldn't understand why and I asked myself how I was going to spend a whole month in this atmosphere. At the bottom, I came across one of the policemen who was guarding the mine, not to prevent theft—there were no problems of that kind—but to make sure that the work ran smoothly and that no fighting broke out. This cop said to me: "Gringo, give me your passport". I told him I didn't have to show him anything because I was Brazilian. At that time, I still had my hair, I was very blond, hair, moustache and beard. The policeman eyed me up and insisted. When I again refused, he handcuffed me and gave me a shove, as though to push me away. Tears sprang to my eyes. Seeing the policeman get angry with me, the workers realized immediately that I was not a spy from the Vale company. I was then taken to a hut where, in the presence of an officer, I had to give an explanation. Realizing the mistake, he apologized and let me go. I went straight back into the mine, where I was given an ovation! In the end, this policeman did me an enormous favour. From then onwards, I felt at home, I could go where I liked and photograph freely. I lived with the miners for several weeks, in the shack belonging to my father's old friend who had known me since childhood.

My photos of this gold mine are quite well known. It is always impressive to see so many people working side by side in an immense open-air hole. My photos manage to convey an idea of the harshness of this work for the miners and thus to arouse a certain empathy, but the people who were working there were all volunteers. They weren't slaves, other than, in a certain way, to their own desires to get rich. They had all arrived there following this dream. Some of them had probably spent their life digging the mine without ever finding gold. But for those who discovered a seam... When, as a result of digging, the miners were getting close to a gold seam, they could see the colour of the earth change. To collect these valuable minerals, the miners of the Serra Pelada did not use ordinary sacks, but white or blue ones. In addition to his normal salary, each carrier of earth had the right to choose a white or blue sack that came from the seam he had discovered. Sifting its contents, he might find five grains or five kilos of gold. It was a lottery.

Among the workers, I met individuals of all types. Some were unable to read or write, while others had studied at university. They were all adventurers, like those who took part in the gold rush in California or Alaska. They regarded the policemen guarding the mine as though they were lackeys

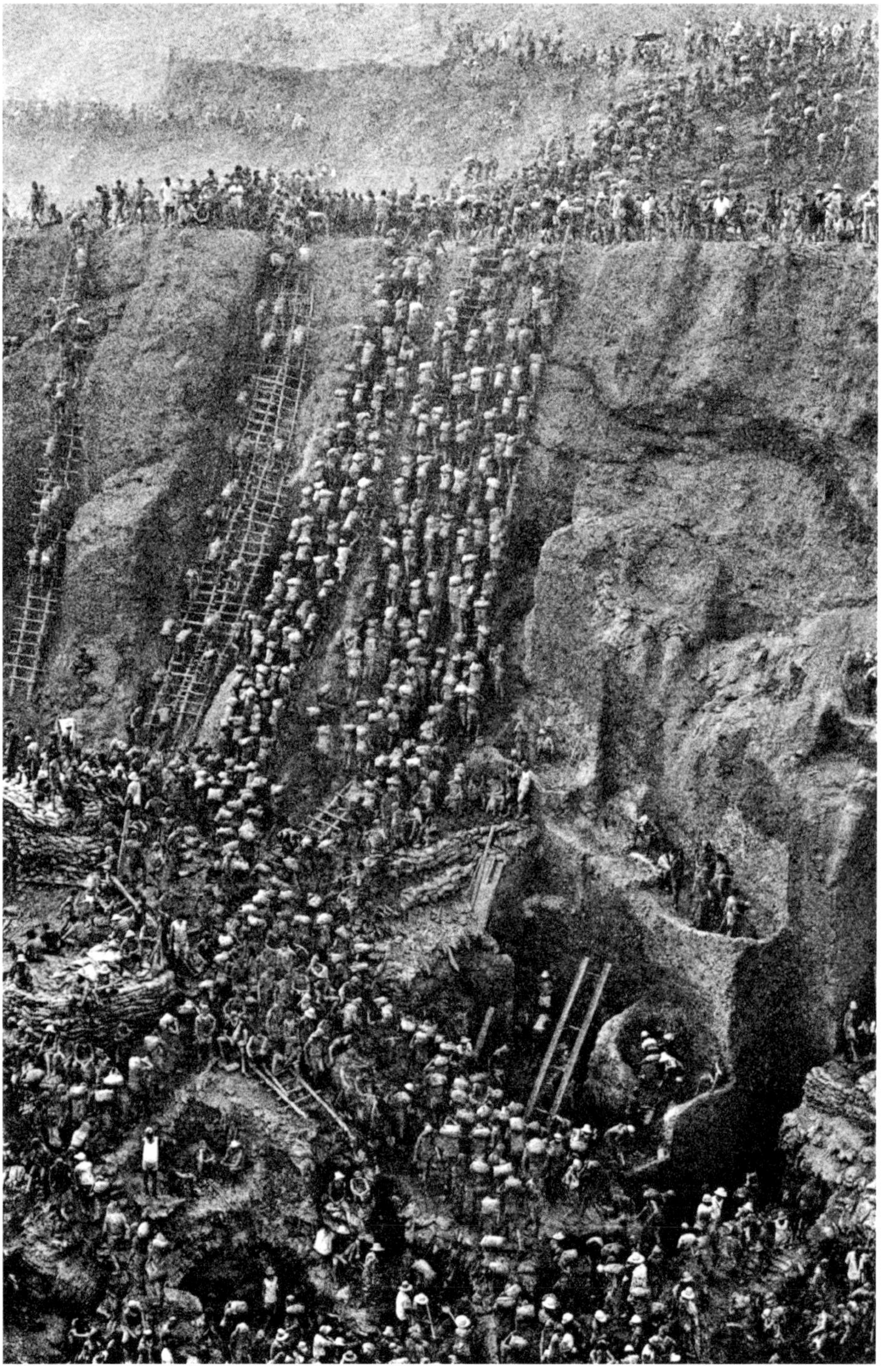

Open-air gold mine, Serra Pelada, State of Pará, Brazil, 1986

who were abusing their power because they had a rifle in their hand. It was truly a class struggle. Whenever a fight broke out, the police didn't hesitate to shoot, sometimes even to kill. But in their turn, they were stoned to death with iron minerals, much heavier than granite.

The workers all lived on site, in shacks where they slept in hammocks. In addition to their salary, they were well fed, with a lot of meat, manioc, rice and vegetables. In my father's friend's shack, boss and workers all ate the same thing. Alcohol was forbidden, there were no women within a range of at least forty or fifty kilometres. A great latent violence reigned, but I also encountered tenderness. In the mine as anywhere else, there were homosexuals. Among the fifty thousand men, a gay organization had even been formed: a sort of small association that added a touch of gentleness. One day, I met a miner, a tough guy who bore the scars of knife wounds. As we were talking, he said: "Sebastião, you are lucky, you live in Paris. My dream, when I find gold, is to go there to have silicone breast implants, that's where the finest ones are". I found it incredible to think that this self-inflicted slavery, in this extremely tough life in the mine, was motivated by his dream of having beautiful silicone breasts. It was so unexpected it made me laugh.

Since then, all the mines have been mechanized in a brutal manner. In 1989, when I was working in the Dhanbad district in India, one hundred and fifty thousand miners were breaking their backs mining coal, working in shifts day and night in tunnels where the temperature rose to 55°C. Until the Second World War, these mines were exploited by the British; at that time, they provided a very good coal for the production of steel. The British had then abandoned them without shutting them down properly. Hence, in certain places, the air circulation caused fire to break out underground. When I was there, the bowels of the earth had been burning for years. There were clouds of smoke everywhere and, passing through the villages, there were places where the ground had subsided. Nevertheless, the inhabitants of the area lived off the mine, about 400,000 people in all. They all had a small plot of land that the women cultivated, while the men worked in the mine, or vice versa. Sometimes, an entire family worked in the mine, as it hired non-skilled labourers, particularly for work on the surface. At that time, they were beginning to set up open-air mines with the aid of enormous Russian machinery: great mechanical shovels, true monsters that could dig and move piles of earth as big as houses. It was definitely the end of an era.

Years later, I returned to this part of Bihar again for my reportages on migrations. I wanted to observe the changes the industrial reorganization had had on the population. The local workforce had been replaced by huge machines; the mine now hired only technicians and other skilled workers. Physical strength had now been replaced by technical knowledge. Many people without qualifications were unemployed and, after having been evicted from their plots of land, these newly impoverished populations had headed for the towns, which had started to expand enormously. I happened to meet families who came to the edge of the mines, at night, to gather fuel. In order to survive, some were forced to steal from the very place that had formerly been their own land. From farmers working in the mines, they had been transformed into proletarians crowded together in the outskirts of the cities, and into thieves who stole from their former property at night. These are the human tragedies resulting from the disappearance of manual labour in the industrial process, which I wanted to relate in my project *Migrations*.

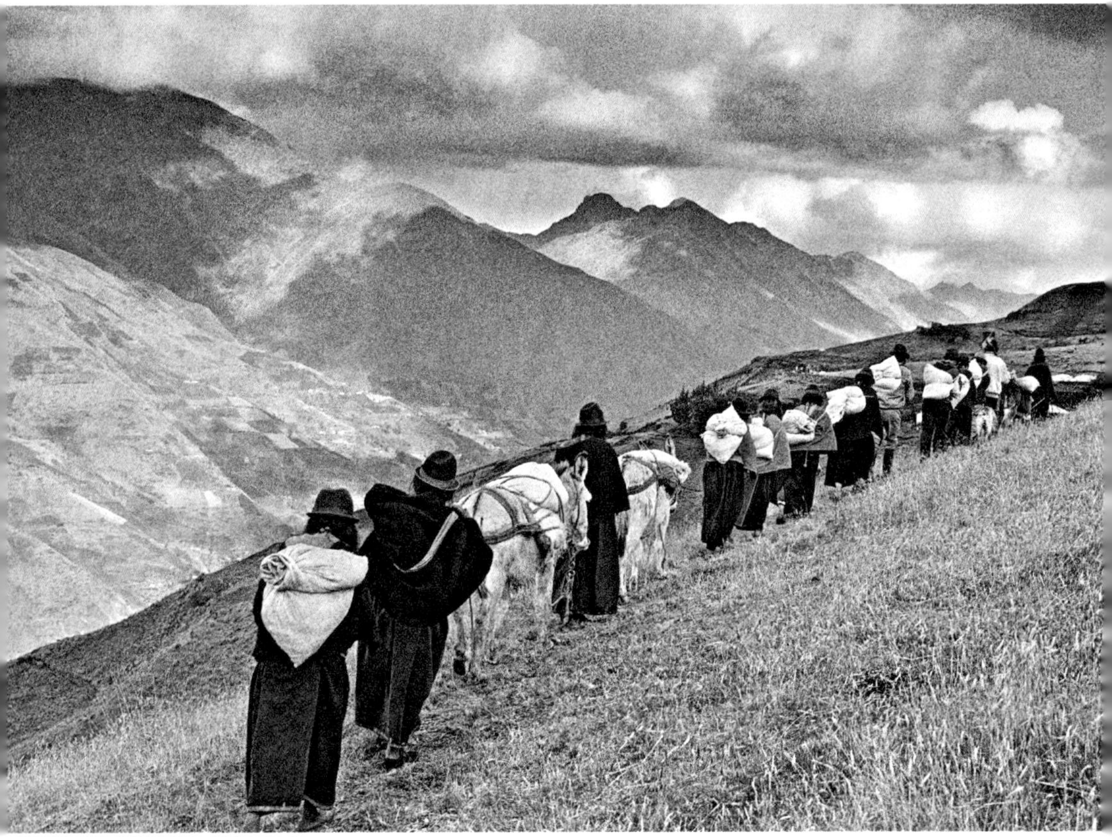

Women carrying produce to market, Chimborazo Province, Ecuador, 1998

Migrations

In 1993, we published the book entitled *Workers*. While we were organizing exhibitions in various museums around the world and I was holding conferences to share my experiences, together with Lélia, I started to conceive a new story: that of the reorganization of the family of man, caused by changes in industry and by the implacable rate of production.

In Bihar, as elsewhere, I had observed the same thing: the delocalization of the great industries of the West towards poorer countries, where labour was cheap, had created hubs of industrial growth that generated enormous movement of population. I don't know what the exact statistics arc today, but during the first half of the Nineties, every year between 150 and 200 million people throughout the world abandoned the countryside for the cities. This movement was in the process of turning the planet upside down. Many of the urban disasters we can see today in the countries of the South are due to these great global shifts in the industrial system. They have generated the new consumer society in the developing countries, the acceleration of the production of cheap goods, population concentration, the emergence of megacities. For the first time in human history, the majority of people live in cities, but most of these new city-dwellers live in terrible conditions.

Cheap labour gathers in the shanty-towns. The scenario is the same everywhere. In the *favelas* of São Paulo or the *ciudades perdidas* in Mexico, we can see the same shacks of wood or corrugated metal, in which families live in cramped conditions. Everywhere, children play amidst piles of rubbish.

All over the planet, the kids who sniff glue or smoke crack are alike; wherever they are, the poor all end up looking the same.

Everywhere in the world, people are displaced more or less for the same economic reasons that benefit a minority, while the majority become poorer. The resulting overpopulation increases the same problems: precariousness, poverty, violence, epidemics. On the threshold of the third millennium, I wanted to show these displaced people and pay tribute to their desire to integrate, their courage in facing being uprooted, their incredible ability to adapt to situations often of extreme difficulty. I wanted to show that, in their own way, they all give a contribution to the world with their spirit of initiative and the wealth of their differences. At the dawn of the twenty-first century, I tried to show the need to re-model the family of man on the basis of solidarity and sharing.

I encountered organizations specializing in these issues and working in close contact with the emigrants, particularly the IOM (International Organization for Migration), based in Geneva, the UNHCR, UNICEF, and so on. Over time, we decided to recount the story of all the populations forced to leave their country for economic reasons, but also religious, climatic or political ones. We christened the project *Exodes* (Migrations).

The need to realize this story grew all the more strongly in us as we found echoes of our own personal story in it. Officially, I had left Brazil to continue my studies in France, but on the date my passport expired, when the Brazilian government had refused to renew it, I was transformed *de facto* into a refugee. In the end, I had obtained French citizenship, as did Lélia and our children, but, unlike our sons who were born in France, I will never be a true Frenchman, but always an immigrant. I am familiar with exile, I know what it means to leave your own country. I have witnessed the anxiety of those who live without papers and I feel an close to anyone who is building a new life far from the land of their birth; with the Salvadoran waiter in a Manhattan restaurant, the Indian shopkeeper in England or the Senegalese worker employed on a construction site in Paris.

Migrations occupied me for six years, during which I travelled in many countries, from India to Latin America, to Iraq. I went to many places that I already knew, starting with Brazil. And everywhere, I observed with great sadness the deterioration in living conditions. I visited the megacities and their shanty-towns, sprawling cities like Shanghai, Jakarta or Mumbai to which an increasing number of migrants in search of work are drawn. I have seen islands of wealth in an ocean of poverty. I shall never forget Manila with its private golf courses while the streets teem with poverty-stricken children. I also remember Vietnamese queuing for hours in front of the United States embassy in Ho Chi Minh City (formerly Saigon), hoping to obtain a visa. Or the "boat people" stranded in Hong Kong, or Galang Island in Indonesia. I came across holds filled with Africans trying to reach Spain illegally to find work. I photographed all these migrants, all these people who faced journeys on land or crowded into boats to search for a better existence elsewhere, often risking their lives.

I also encountered people struck by natural disasters, like the inhabitants of Honduras whose villages had been flooded in the aftermath of Hurricane Mitch in 1998. These areas had already experienced storms in the past, and the inhabitants had seen their homes carried away by mudslides.

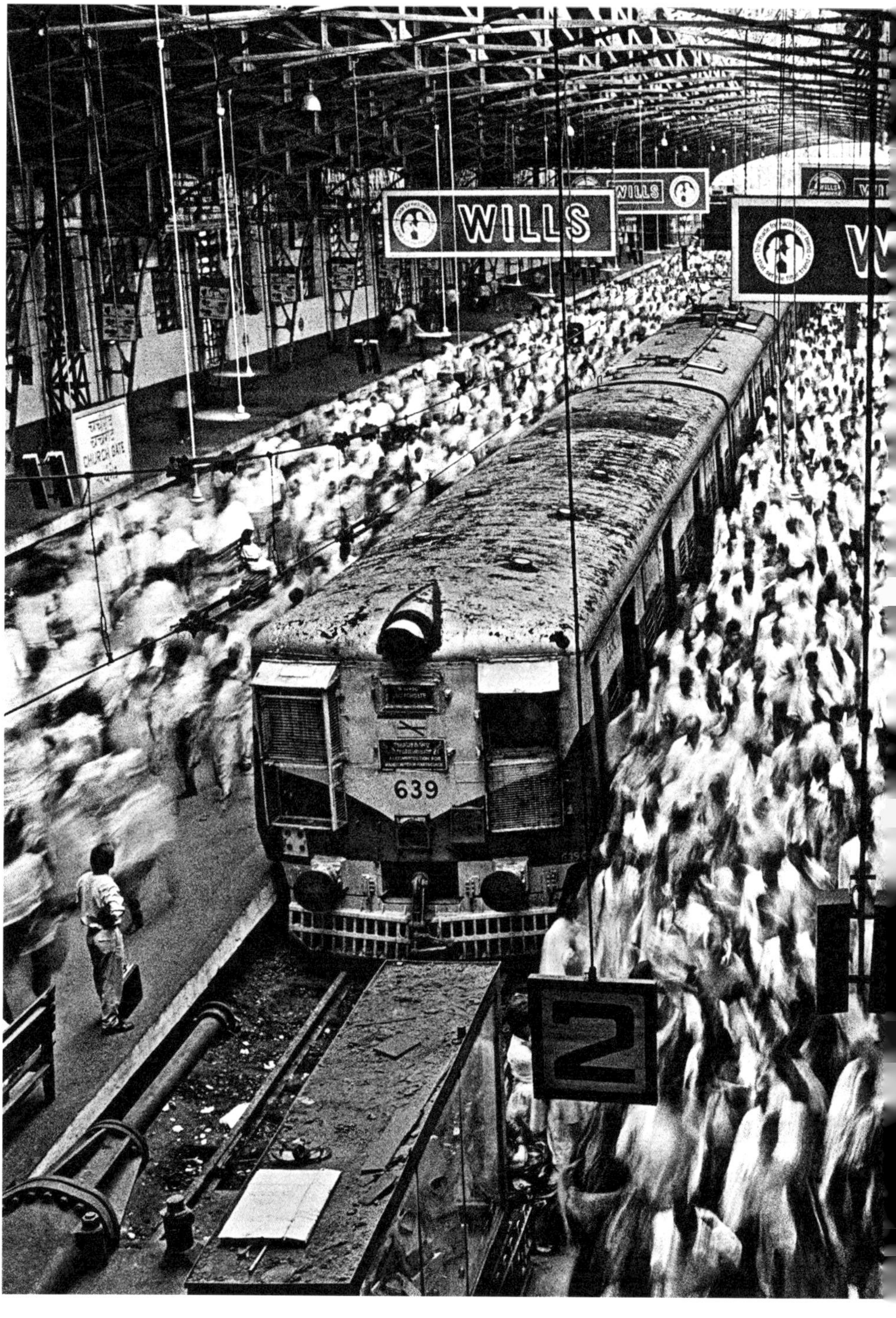
WILLS
WILLS
CHURCH GATE
639
2

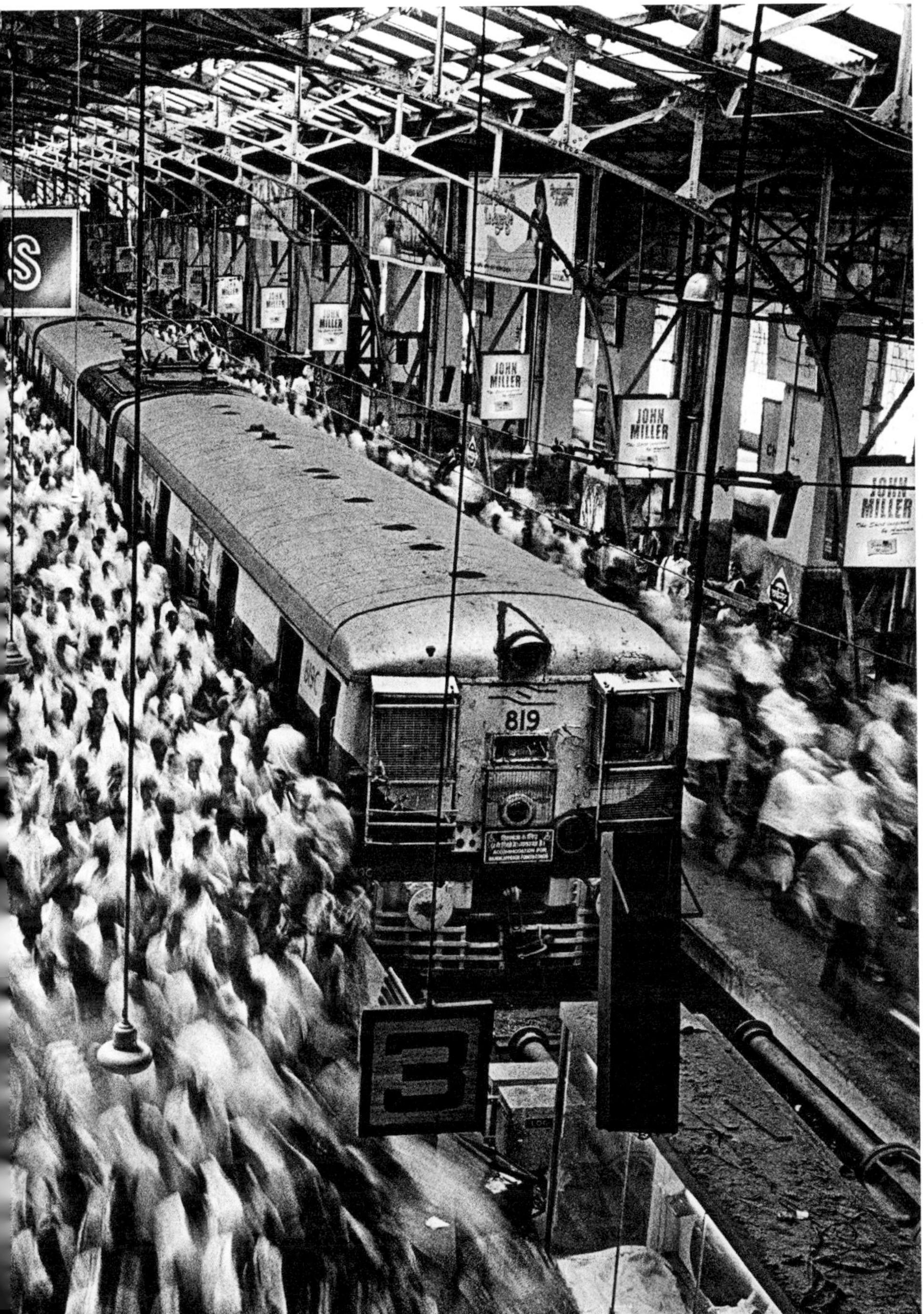

Churchgate Station, Bombay (Mumbai), India, 1995

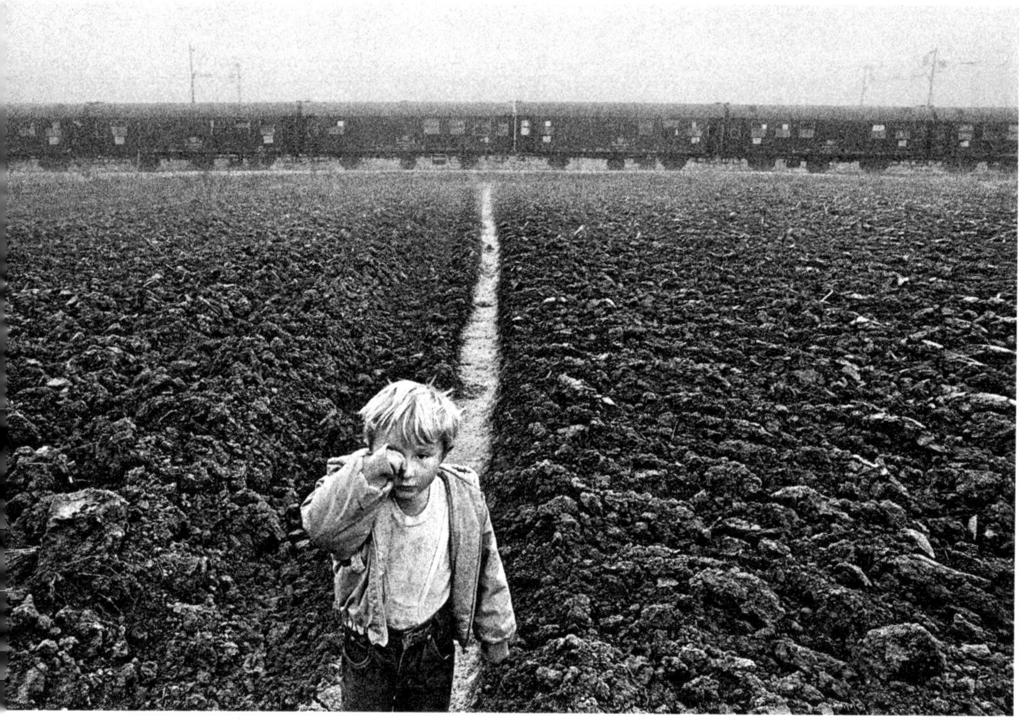

Ivanko railway station, 120 refugees living in a train, Croatia, 1994

But until then, the roots of the trees had always held onto the soil. This time, deforestation, the intervention of man, had worsened the effects of the catastrophe. I also visited populations under threat, like the Kurds in Iraq, and went into refugee camps in Afghanistan and elsewhere. Unlike the migrants, they were not dreaming of finding a better life. It was the fear of repression or war that had forced them to leave, then they tried the best they could to adapt to life in the camps. Some ended up by becoming permanent residents, like the Palestinians in Lebanon. Many never returned home and became migrants.

I also went to the Balkans, where I met people who were disoriented, and had been set against each other by deceitful and belligerent warlords. Millions of former Yugoslavs who had now become as many Croats, Serbs and Bosnians, all enemies of each other, forced to flee the places in which they had always lived. There, I also came across Gypsies who were persecuted. Then I saw the exodus of the Albanians and the Kosovans. The similarity of all these situations began to weigh me down.

These reportages set me before the victims of our world and its various mechanisms who, in the end, are all very alike and have many things in common. These people were going through terrible moments, sometimes the worst in their lives, yet they allowed me to photograph them. I think they wanted their plight to be known.

In the end, this story, which I initially thought I knew like the back of my hand, deeply shocked and overwhelmed me. Emotionally and also in my beliefs. In the course of my various reportages, I had witnessed so many tragedies that I believed I was now accustomed, but I hadn't expected to encounter such violence, hatred and brutality. I did not think that ethnic cleansing could still take place in Europe: I could never have imagined the nightmare of the Balkans. And then the massacres and genocide that I subsequently discovered in Africa reached such levels of atrocity that it was impossible to emerge from it emotionally unscathed, or without feeling deeply uneasy about the future of humanity.

Mozambique: the long road back

In 1992, the United Nations obtained a peace agreement between the two enemy factions who, since 1976, had been engaged in a bloody, all-out civil war in Mozambique. Some time later, happy about the truce, I decided to visit this former Portuguese colony in southern Africa. I wanted to witness the return of the hundreds of thousands of Mozambican refugees who, for many years, had been living in camps in Malawi, Zimbabwe and South Africa.

For a better understanding of the situation, it is necessary to go back to independence, won in 1975 by Frelimo (the Frente de Libertação de Moçambique, or Mozambican Liberation Front) following a long struggle. After having prevailed over the Portuguese, Frelimo established a Marxist-Leninist government. Its great neighbour South Africa, still under the yoke of the extreme right government responsible for the creation of the apartheid regime, terrified at the idea that these movements might contaminate its own masses of black workers, had hastened to provoke a guerilla war in Mozambique. South Africa had thus created and financed Renamo (Resistência Nacional Moçambicana, or Mozambican National Resistance), which became an extremely powerful movement.

Just like at the time of the war of independence, one group (Renamo) held the countryside, and the other (Frelimo) the towns. The Cold War then came into the conflict, since the Western bloc supported South Africa, while the USSR supported Mozambique. When Renamo entered the villages to massacre the population, most of the adults were working in the fields and the kids were at school. So those who were able to flee did so, every man for himself. During this escape, families were divided, separated. When Renamo captured the children, they enrolled them and turned them into child soldiers. This period was marked by unspeakable violence.

At the end of this civil war, humanitarian organizations such as UNICEF, the World Health Organization, MSF, the UNHCR, IOM and the Save the Children Fund, with whom I was working, ran the refugee camps. Some contained five thousand, at times ten thousand lost children; others were occupied by adults and families. To help parents and children locate each other again, photographic portraits proved extremely useful. It was necessary to be very careful beforc entrusting kids to adults who were returning home, some tried to abduct the children to reduce them to slavery. The organizations thus undertook a large tracing programme, thanks to which thousands of children were reunited with their families.

During the weeks I spent in the refugee camps, I noticed that individuals from both sides, Renamo and Frelimo, were living there together. All had been similarly forced from their homes and the conflict had left them starving. These enemy populations who had recently been engaged in an unusually violent war, were now reunited in the same camps. To make co-habitation possible, ceremonies of exorcism were organized. I witnessed moments of great intensity in which the participants hurled themselves against the spirits of war, armed with rifles and knives between their teeth. Once the spirits had been chased away, a single Mozambican people remained and could return home. It was incredibly moving to be on those buses, trucks, or on foot, alongside all these people who, until a few weeks earlier, had been fighting each other in a merciless war…

I marched long distances with these populations. Kilometres and kilometres, between Malawi and Mozambique. I realized that these people, who had lived crammed into camps of fifty thousand, one hundred thousand, two hundred thousand refugees, had just experienced an almost urban way of living. For years, all these country people had lived in groups of huts, separated by passageways identical to animated streets full of life. In the camps, there were also schools and a small hospital. As the months went by, these country folk had turned into townsfolk. Returning to Mozambique, the majority no longer wanted to live in the countryside and ended up by swelling the numbers in the towns. This war radically changed their way of life.

On the road back, I witnessed some harsh scenes, particularly beside the Zambezi. I remember people who reached the riverbanks at night, thirsty, dirty, and threw themselves into the water without noticing the crocodiles, hidden in the dark. Some were caught… it was terrible. I also remember an incredible episode, amusing and dramatic at the same time. Crossing the Dona Ana bridge, the longest river bridge in the world measuring some 13 kilometres and destroyed here and there by the war, I came across a woman laden with bags and with her baby on her back. I asked her if she was going to Vila de Sena, on the other side of the bridge. Laughing, she explained to me that she was going much further. So I asked her if she was heading for Beira, a town about 300 kilometres away. She replied: “No, I'm going to Maputo”, in other words she was about to cover another 1,250 kilometres on foot with all her baggage and her baby. I will never forget the calmness and determination of this woman, nor her courage. I am sure she reached her destination.

I went back to Mozambique several times. In April 1994, in the middle of one of these trips, I went to join Lélia for a few days in Brazil. I then left again at the beginning of May from São Paulo for Maputo, via South Africa. During the stopover at Johannesburg airport, I suddenly heard my name over the loudspeaker: I was to call Lélia as soon as possible. On the phone, she told me: "Don't go to Mozambique, go to Rwanda. Tens of thousands of people are fleeing to Tanzania…"

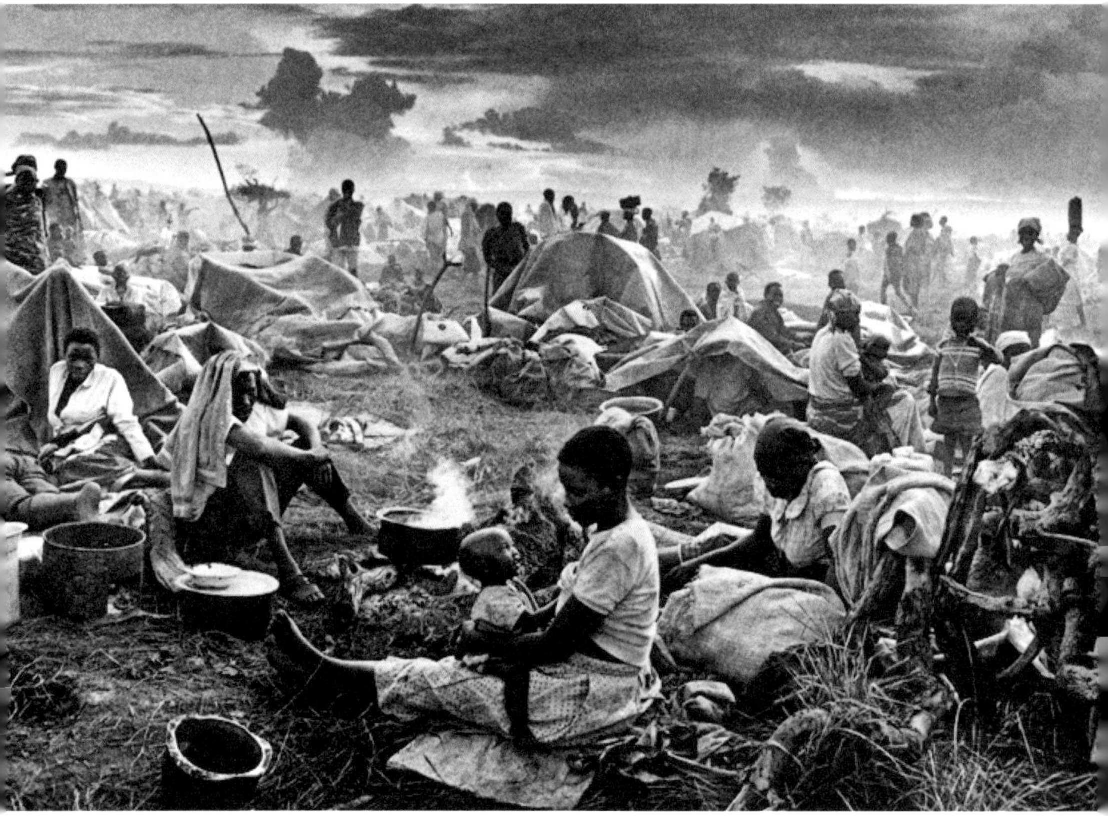

Rwandan refugee camp, Benako, Tanzania, 1994

Rwanda

So, rather than returning to Mozambique as planned, I bought a ticket for Kenya, as this was the only way to reach Rwanda. On arrival in Nairobi, I went to the offices of the UNHCR, who I was working for. There, I was told that I could no longer enter Rwanda: a war was about to break out and tens of thousands of people were fleeing towards Tanzania. They suggested I should catch a plane that very evening and head for that border. By the time I disembarked in Benako, in northeast Tanzania, one hundred thousand refugees were there already. Within a few days, this number had risen to a million. As for the dead... It is not necessary to remind anyone that, in 1994, Rwanda became thc thcatre of one of the worst genocides of the twentieth century.

In the midst of this disaster, I immediately set to work. I saw terrible things, some of them unforgettable. Near the Akagera, the river that separates Tanzania from Rwanda, I saw dozens and dozens of bodies floating beneath a small bridge. There was a waterfall over which the corpses dropped continuously, before being sucked into a whirlpool. It was awful.

At one point, I came upon some Tutsi guerrillas who had recaptured that particular part of Rwanda, while the Hutus were in Kigali, backed by French forces, with a zone behind the front reaching as far as the border with the Congo. These Tutsis told me that they had a car and could take me to Kigali, if I wanted. We set out, and had to cover about 150 kilometres. The road was strewn with mutilated, dismembered bodies. Whenever we stopped for a break, we walked through the piles of bodies stacked beneath the banana trees.

The photos I took are horrific. This war broke out on the pretext of ethnicity. But there were other factors: a history of poverty, exploitation. I had already been aware of this for a long time.

I first got to know Rwanda in 1971, when I worked there for the International Coffee Organization. In 1991, I went back there again, for *Workers*, wanting to revisit those village tea plantations (as these family-run small plantations were known) I had helped to create. I remembered all those small producers who were working at a loss, morning till night, to produce the best and most expensive tea in the world. After 1971, the population had increased enormously, while the slice of the cake became increasingly small. This growing poverty turned cancerous in a society divided by the racial tensions between Hutus and Tutsis. In addition, in 1975, when the Mouvement républicain national pour le dévelopement (MRND, or National Republican Movement for Development) came to power, establishing a government that was very strict, France had signed an aid agreement with Rwanda, on the pretext of its proximity and close ties to the French-speaking countries. Not to build schools there, however, but barracks. Between 1987 and 1994, France thus sent military equipment to the country on a regular basis. All these factors contributed to creating a volatile situation that eventually exploded, creating the chaos I discovered in 1994. I subsequently returned to Mozambique to continue my work with the humanitarian organizations, but Rwanda became an obsession for me and I went back there on many other occasions.

After the massacre of the Tutsis perpetrated by the Hutus, the Tutsi forces recaptured Kigali. The majority of Hutus fled to Zaire (now the Democratic Republic of Congo), Tanzania and Burundi. It was a disaster: eventually, over two million people found themselves living in refugee camps. I watched them arrive in groups, trying to survive there, one on top of another. Problems of hygiene soon erupted. The humanitarian organizations were overwhelmed, completely powerless due to a lack of equipment and medicines. Cholera broke out immediately in Zaire.

I saw strong people, warriors, completely drained in the space of a few hours and dropping like flies. Due to the overcrowded conditions, these infectious diarrheas spread at the speed of light, killing thousands of people every day. It was not even possible to bury the bodies, which were piled up one on top of another. I saw heaps of corpses stretching for hundreds of metres. The French army came with a bulldozer to dig communal graves. A mechanical shovel picked up ten to fifteen bodies at a time and put them in the ditch, sometimes leaving behind an arm, a head or a leg. It was madness. The survivors seemed to have become immune to it all, but I began to feel as though I was dying. The nine months I spent in Rwanda were so shocking that at a certain point my mind and body started to give way. I was being attacked by my own Staphylococcus and my doctor in Paris finally ordered me to rest in order to get well again.

A few months later, in 1995, when I had fully recovered, I returned to Kigali to continue my reportage. I looked for my friend Joseph Munyankindi, but he had been murdered with his wife and their children. It was a terrible shock. We had met on my first trip to Rwanda, when I was a young economist working for the International Coffee Organization and he was the director of the Office of Industrial Culture in Rwanda. We had covered hundreds of miles in his Beetle, looking for sites where tea plantations could be established. We talked and laughed together and became good friends. We had met again in London, I had introduced him to Lélia, he had come to our house. I had visited him every time I had passed through Kigali and had always been welcomed with open arms. He had introduced me to his wife: he was Hutu, she a Tutsi of extraordinary beauty. When I went back there for *Workers* in 1991, three and a half years before the situation exploded, my eldest son Juliano, then aged 17, came with me. During that visit, we could already sense enormous tension.

When we tried to hire a car to go to the Kivu region to see the famous tea plantations, the international companies were no longer hiring their vehicles to anyone leaving the capital. Joseph Munyankindi had managed to get hold of a friend's Peugeot 304 for us. We went through sixteen checkpoints along the route to Bukavu, close to the border with the Congo. When we got there, we started to work, I on my photos, Juliano on an essay he had to prepare for school. Every three or four days, we spoke to the person who had rented us the car, then to his wife. Then, we were no longer able to reach them. Returning to Kigali, Munyankindi informed us that the owner of the car had been murdered. Hutu police had burst into his house, thinking they would find money there and had killed him.

During the same period, Joseph Munyankindi's wife had been imprisoned for the second time; as a Tutsi, she was suspected of spying. Before our departure, my friend gave us some letters to post to Germany. At the time, he was no longer working for the government, but for Misereor, a German Christian organization that supported development projects. He did not dare to post those letters himself. I had sensed that he was very worried. I did not realize that it would be the last time I saw him. I lost my friend in the bloodbath that was the genocide.

Returning to the famous tea plantations where I had been so happy, firstly with him, and then with Juliano, I found that everything was burnt. Nothing remained of the tea that had been so difficult to plant and cultivate. On the devastated ground, bones were strewn everywhere. Perhaps those remains were of people we had known and with whom we had spent such happy times…

It is strange how certain parts of the world leave a profound mark on each of us. As a young economist, I travelled the length and breadth of Rwanda, looking for the incredibly fertile soils of Kivu. As a photographer, I returned there for *Workers*. In 1994, I witnessed total disaster. In 1995, I went back again to observe the return of the refugees. For my next project, *Genesis*, I wanted to photograph the volcanoes in eruption near Goma and the gorillas in Virunga National Park. I have been to and fro to Rwanda for very different reasons and in very different circumstances. How many times? I don't know exactly, but always to the same place. Without ever having truly decided it, many of my stories took place there, near Lake Kivu.

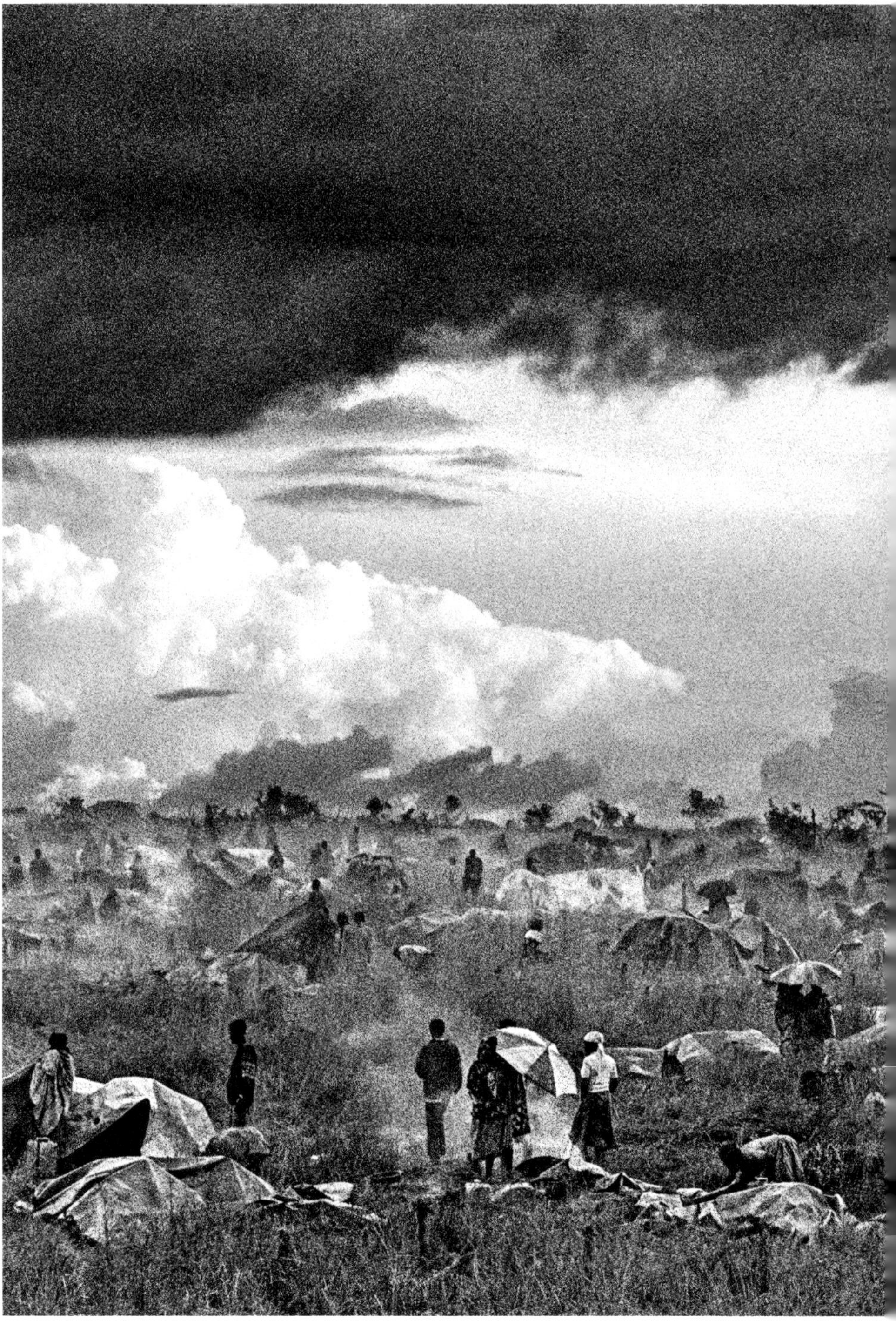

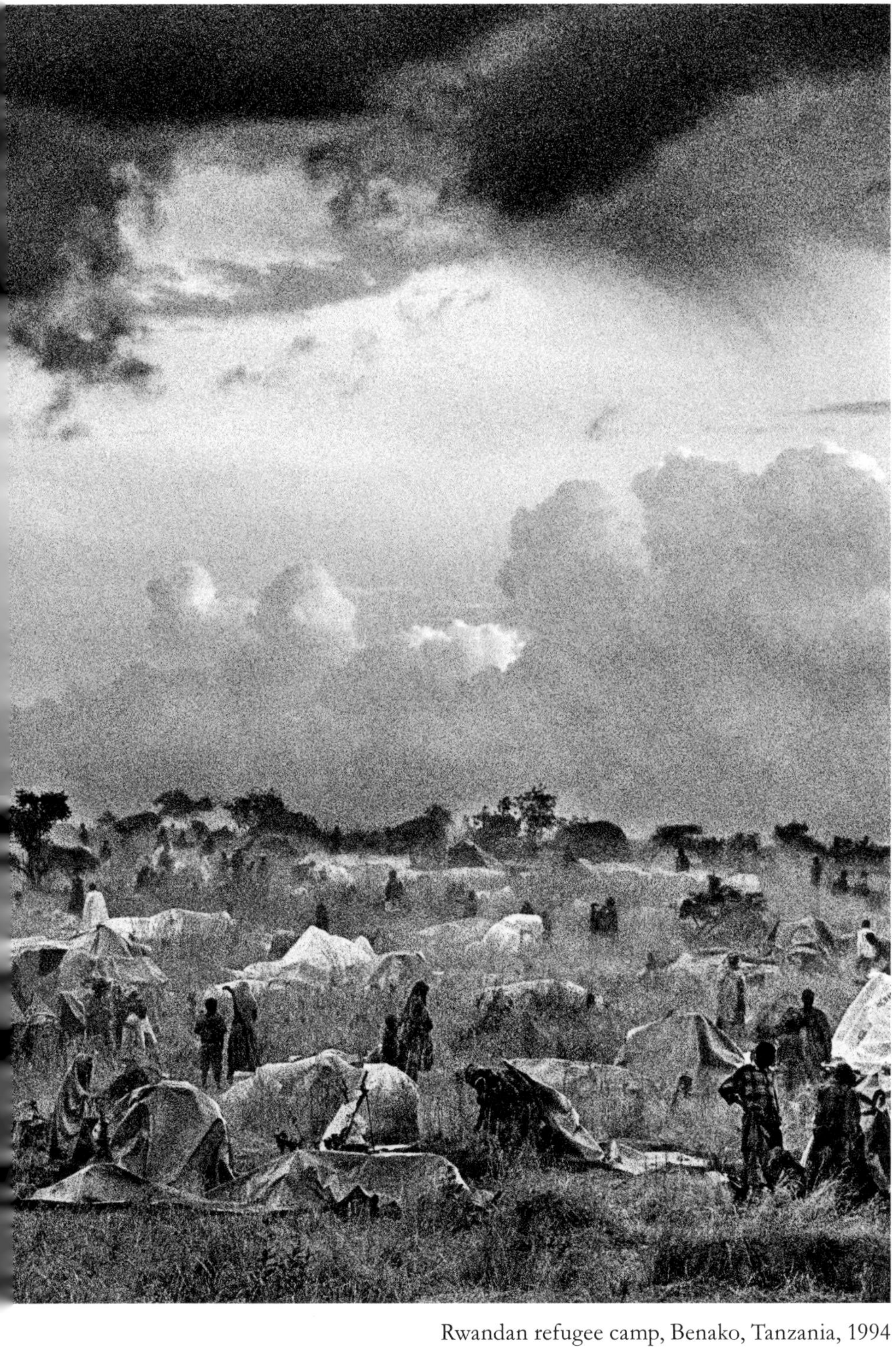

Rwandan refugee camp, Benako, Tanzania, 1994

Looking death in the face

As I have already said, I saw so much suffering, hatred and violence in the course of my reportages for *Migrations*, that I emerged from it extremely shaken. But I have no regrets about doing them. I am sometimes asked: "When you are faced with such atrocities, what is a good photo?" My reply is concise: photography is my language. The photographer is there to keep his mouth shut, whatever the situation. His task is to look and to photograph. It is through photography that I work, express myself and live.

I love Rwanda. I wanted to photograph its workers and its plantations, the beauty of its parks, as well as the atrocities that took place there, for this very reason—I love it. And at that horrific time, I photographed it with all my heart. I thought the whole world needed to know. No one has the right to protect himself from the tragedies of his time, because we are all responsible, in a certain way, for what happens in the society in which we have chosen to live.

We have to recognize that this consumer society, to which we all belong, exploits and impoverishes many of the planet's inhabitants. We all have a duty to keep ourselves informed about the tragedies arising from the inequalities between North and South and the string of disasters this engenders, through radio, television, reading the papers and looking at photos. This is our world, we have to assume responsibility for it. Disasters are not created by photographers, but are the symptoms of the dysfunctions of this world of which we are all part. Photographers are there to act as mirrors, just like journalists. So don't talk to me about voyeurism! The voyeurs are the politicians who stood idly by and the military who facilitated the repression in Rwanda. They are responsible, together with the United Nations Security Council, which, with all its failings, could not prevent millions of people from being murdered.

I have always tried to show people in all their dignity. In the majority of cases, they are the victims of cruelty, of events. They are photographed at a time in which they have lost their homes, seen their loved ones murdered, sometimes even their own children. For the most part, they are innocent people who do not deserve the misfortunes that have struck them. I took these photos because I thought that everyone needed to know. That is my opinion, but I don't force anyone to look at them. I am not here to lecture or to set my conscience at rest by arousing feelings of compassion. I took these images because I had a moral, ethical obligation to do so. In such moments of suffering, you may ask, what are morals, what are ethics? It is when I am faced with someone who is dying and I have to decide whether or not to release the shutter of my camera.

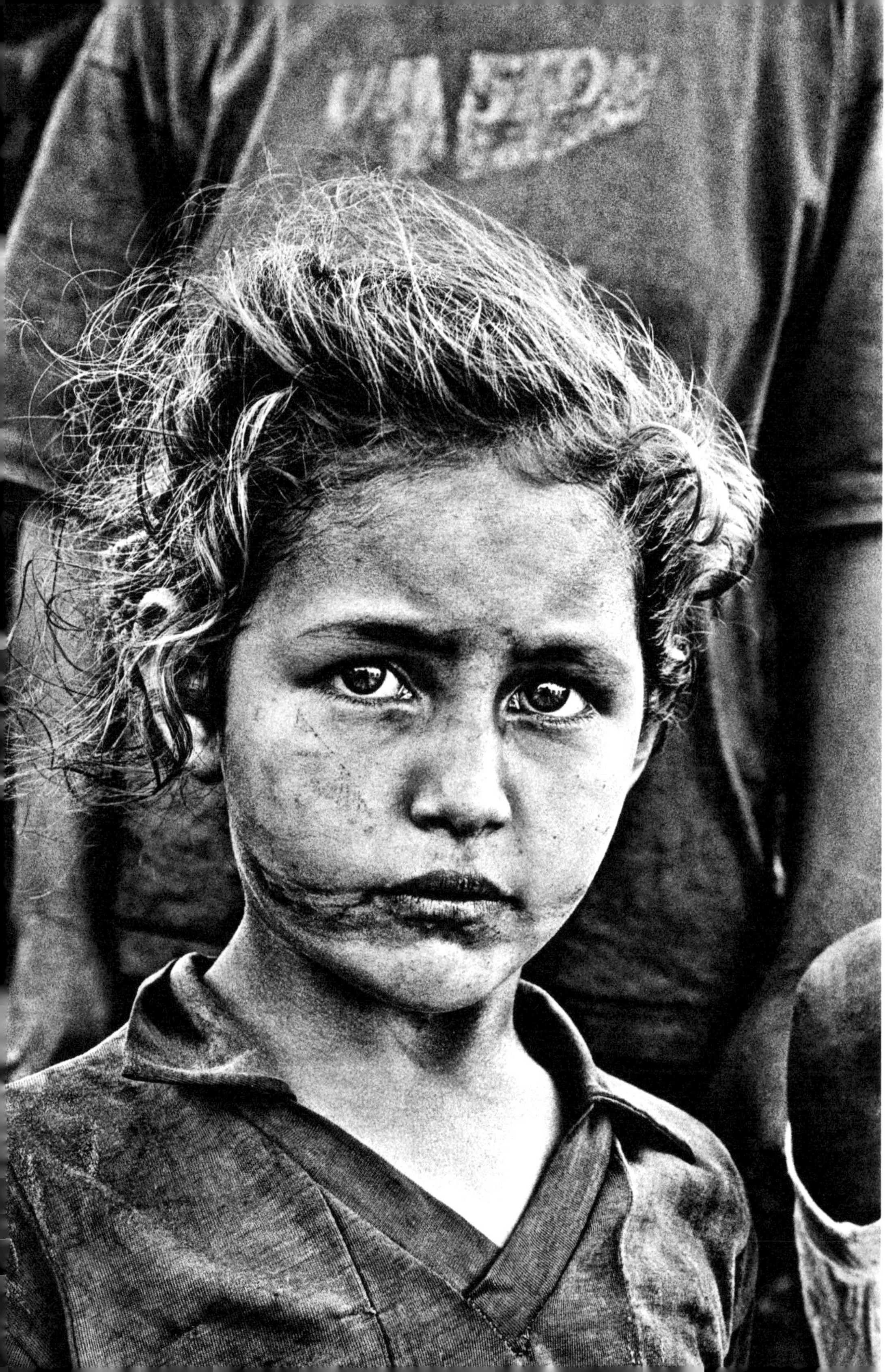

Instituto Terra: the realization of utopia

In 2000, we published two books, *Migrations* and *The Children*. While more often than not displaced peoples are victims, their children are so to an even greater extent. They often display a great ability to adapt, to play games, to laugh. But in all these scrawny, dirty, wounded or maimed children, it was their gaze that struck me most of all. I dedicated the book we devoted to them "to all the children who look at these photographs and are moved to think about the lives behind the faces."

The photos I took for *Migrations* went all round the world and were seen by thousands of people, exhibited in many museums and galleries and published in magazines across the globe. I also held many conferences. At that time, however, I was not well, either physically or psychologically. Until then, I had never imagined that man could be part of a species capable of such cruelty to its own members and I couldn't accept it. I was depressed and was sinking into a deeply pessimistic state of mind. I was equally despairing about how economic, social and political upheavals had altered the planet. The felled trees, the ruined landscapes, the destruction of entire ecosystems... So I dreamed of setting up a project that would denounce pollution and the destruction of the forests. In the meantime, Lélia had had the brilliant idea of replanting the forest on the damaged land we had been given by my parents in 1990, in Brazil. We threw ourselves into this crazy venture and then, suddenly, the trees came to life again.

Paraná, Brazil, 1996

When the Portuguese arrived in the sixteenth century, 3,500 kilometres of the Brazilian coastline were covered with

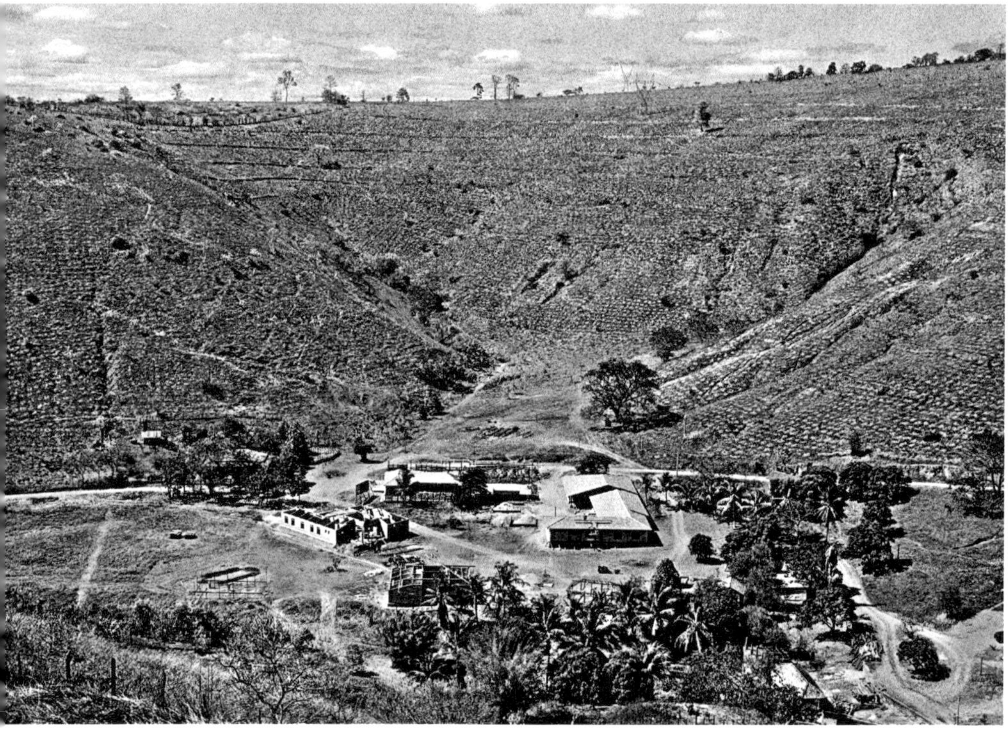

Instituto Terra, 2001

Atlantic forest, reaching about 350 kilometres inland: an area twice the size of France. My parents' land was part of this ecosystem. When Lélia and I were able to return to our country following the political amnesty, we realized that all the trees had been cut down. The famous *perobas*, cousins of the oak, and many other species, had been used to furnish the housing in Brazil's cities, which were rapidly expanding at the time, and to produce wood coal for the steel industry. Thanks to deforestation, the rain water now flowed directly away, with nothing to hold it back any longer, and my parents' fertile land, once covered with pastures, rice paddies and forest, was now a bare crust. Of the thirty or so families who lived there when I was a child, only the cowherd remained. Each time we went back, we witnessed the speed of this process increase.

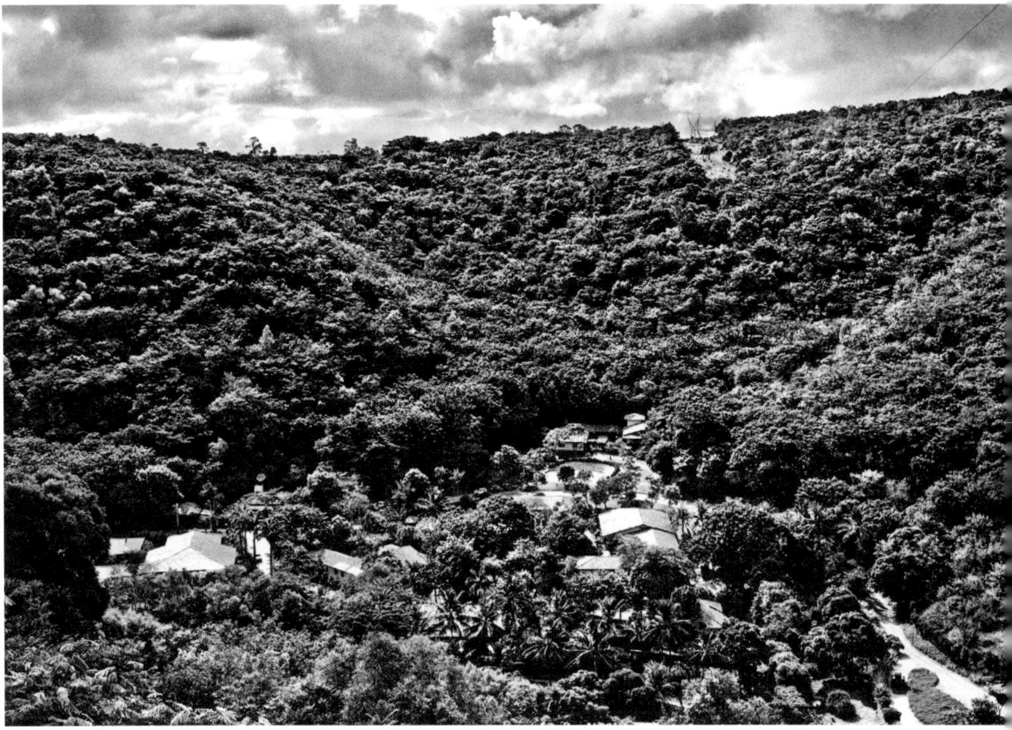

Instituto Terra, 2013

Faced with this disaster, one day Lélia announced: "Sebastião, we are going to replant it." We had no financial interest in doing this, we didn't live there and we had no idea how much a tree might cost. But we decided to try our luck. We went to see Renato de Jesus, an engineer famous for his work in the recovery of ecosystems, who came to examine the state of our land, the condition of its soil. Within six months, he presented us with a plan: the replanting of 2.5 million trees! In addition, it was necessary to ensure that there would be biodiversity. At least two hundred different species were needed to re-establish the ecosystem. We had no idea how to go about doing this, or find the financing for it, but we said: "Let's just get on with it". This engineer with his enthusiasm for reforestation assured us that we would be given lots of help, considering the importance of re-establishing ecosystems. I went to Washington, to a meeting with the World Bank. Those I met thought the idea completely mad and very amusing. Nevertheless, they put us in touch with an interesting network of Brazilian environmentalists. Its members were almost all based in my state, Minas Gerais. Thus we discovered another "madman", the director of the parks and forests of Minas Gerais, Célio Murilo Vale, who straightaway was incredibly enthusiastic and promised to help us. Together, we created the first national park in Brazil on land that was completely damaged, solely on the basis of our promise to replant using species of the native forest. By now, my parents' land was protected. It had become a Private Natural Heritage Reserve and could never be used as agricultural land again. Initially, my father was sceptical about our project. He was convinced that our city-dweller's utopia would ruin us. But when he died at the age of ninety-five, he had had time to see the trees reclaim their rights.

To finance the project, we decided to devote to it the fruits of our labour. The directors of the local mining company, Vale do Rio Doce (now Vale), for which Renato de Jesus worked, also thought our idea was mad, but agreed to help us all the same. Having created a plant nursery to cover their requirements as far as reforestation with native species was concerned, they gave us some small plants and placed some workers at our disposal. They also allocated us some funds, as did the Fondo Brasileño para la Biodiversidad, which was working with the World Bank. Most of our support came from the Federal Government of Brazil, as well as from the states of Minas Gerais and Espírito Santo. Many Brazilian companies and foundations also helped us, just as we were able to count on substantial support from enterprises and foundations in France and Monte Carlo, the government of Asturias and the Generalitat Valenciana in Spain; in Italy, we received support from the Emilia-Romagna region, the Province of Rome, the Friuli region and the city of Parma. In this way, we have already succeeded in replanting two million trees of over three hundred different species. And this is only the beginning. We hope that by 2050, not only will the reforestation of our nature reserve be complete, but that we will be able to help to plant more than fifty million trees in the great valley adjacent to us.

In November 1999, at the end of the rainy season, when we planted the first trees, to be honest I did not believe that even one plant would flourish. By mid-2000, however, we had some shoots measuring 70 centimetres. A bush is like a baby; when it is born it is, in effect, a human being. A baby needs love, protection, it has to learn to walk, but it already possesses all the emotions of a human being. It is the same for a bush: at six months, when it measures only 70 centimetres, it already has the structures of a fully-grown tree. Insects come to feed off its tiny flowers and when its tiny leaves fall to the ground, the ants grab them. It is already a whole world. Lélia always used to say "We have a baby forest", but it was a forest already.

By now we have our own plant nursery, and we supply bushes to the states of Minas Gerais and Espírito Santo. Our nursery has a capacity of a million plants a year, of over a hundred different species. Around what was formerly the corral, new buildings have sprung up and now contain an environmental education centre, the Instituto Terra,[1]

1. www.institutoterra.org

welcoming forest rangers, farmers, mayors, drivers of the municipal bulldozers. It also welcomes children from local schools, raising awareness in them early about the problems of deforestation, and teaching them about the importance of biodiversity and the need to rebuild the ecosystem.

Many animals have returned, even the jaguar, the largest creature in the food chain in our forest. If it has come back, it means that there is enough for it to eat and the food chain is therefore complete. Now, the land has become almost more beautiful than when I was a child. I was completely enchanted before this spectacle and it was not long before Lélia and I decided that we needed to realize a photographic essay showing the beauty of the world. The beginning of everything, for, in recreating this forest, we were in the process of recreating a life cycle.

We made enquiries at the largest NGO for environmental conservation, Conservation International in Washington, which monitors all the world's virgin territories, and discovered that roughly 46% of the planet has been preserved. Humans have destroyed well over half the planet, which is unbelievable, but the other half, or almost, is intact, which seemed fantastic to me. Part of the Amazon rainforest has, effectively, been destroyed, but 75% of it still remains, most of it in Brazil. All over the world, parts of the rainforest have been destroyed, but that does not prevent a large portion from surviving. And then all the places that are difficult to reach have escaped destruction by man, deserts and cold places, in the South as well as the North. 99.9% of Antarctica is virgin territory, as are regions situated above altitudes of 3,000 metres, too difficult to develop.

Gradually, after much reflection and discussion, we put our project together. Then, we began to look for funding. We drew up exclusive contracts with a series of magazines, such as *Paris Match* in France, *Rolling Stone* in the United States, *La Vanguardia* in Spain, *Visão* in Portugal, *The Guardian* in the United Kingdom and *La Repubblica* in Italy. Initially, we planned to finance the project with these contracts and the publications that would follow in the course of eight years' work. But the press was in financial difficulties due to the rise of the internet and we had to look for other sponsors. So we were also helped by American foundations and other enterprises, such as Vale, our Brazilian partner.

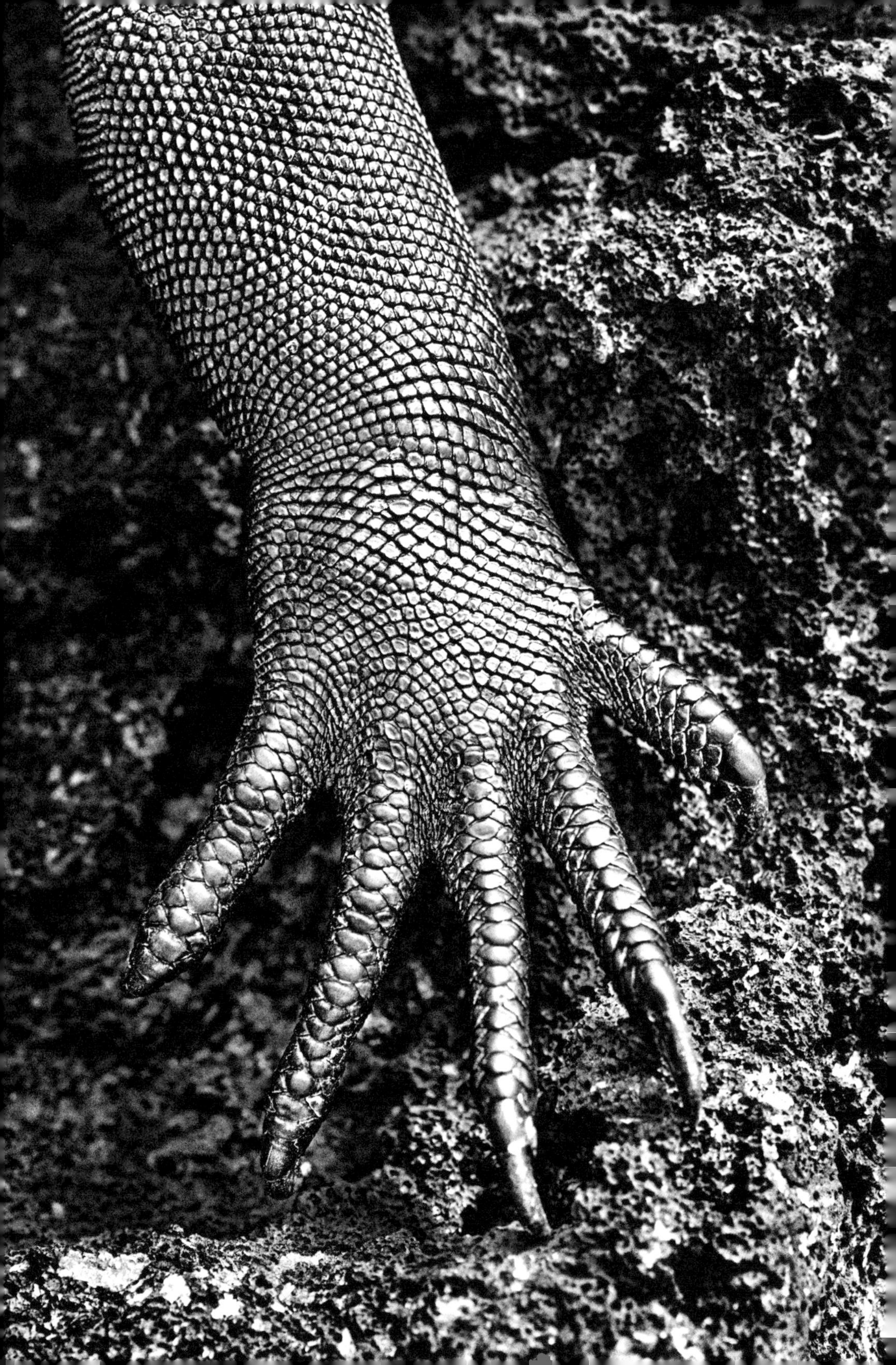

Back to the beginning

In 2002, the idea of *Genesis* was born. It was therefore necessary to plan, in concrete terms, the thirty-two reportages I was to carry out in the untouched areas of the planet, from the hottest to the coldest, the driest to the most lush. As far as my personal preparation was concerned, with the passing of the years and all my experience, I was well run-in. I have four large crates that contain everything I need to live at -30°C, at altitude, in places that are humid or those as hot as an oven. With time, I have acquired my own view about what is essential. In the first place, all my photographic equipment: my cameras and, for a long time, the little suitcase in which my films were neatly packed, safe and sound.

When I started *Genesis*, I had no assistants. As for all my other photographic expeditions, it was therefore necessary to be able to carry everything. When I set off, on the 4th the January 2004, to carry out my first reportage in the Galápagos, I found a guide there, although I had left Paris alone. In Antarctica, in 2005, while I was travelling on the schooner *Tara*[1] with Gil Kebaïli, a reporter for the *Ushuaïa* programme on the French TV channel TF1, he convinced me to stop travelling on my own because this kind of reportage calls for many rules on safety. I noticed, in fact, that while walking on glaciers, it takes nothing to fall into a deep crevasse.

Marine iguana,
Galápagos Islands,
Ecuador, 2004

1. *Tara* is a schooner, captained by Etienne Bourgois, whose mission is the exploration and defence of the environment. From September 2006 to February 2008, to mark International Polar Year, it sailed the Arctic Ocean to observe phenomena associated with climate change.

He persuaded me to hire an assistant. On my return, I met Jacques Barthélemy, a mountain guide; he taught me how to walk, climb and to use ropes and harnesses. He subsequently accompanied me on most of my reportages.

Lélia and I had meticulously planned the eight years I was going to be spending travelling the world on foot, in small aircrafts, boats, canoes and even a hot air balloon—one of my most wonderful memories. After having devoted so many years to depicting men, women and children and their daily life, now I was going to be photographing volcanoes, dunes, glaciers, forests, rivers, canyons, whales, reindeer, lions, pelicans, the world of the jungle, the desert and the ice fields.

It was also a great pleasure to return to Africa on several occasions, no longer to witness tragedies, but this time to capture its extraordinary beauty. I also walked in the Sahara. I visited some of the planet's natural sanctuaries, especially islands. I have already mentioned the Galápagos, but I also went to Madagascar, Sumatra, the Mentawi islands, where the natural environment has been remarkably preserved, to New Guinea and West Papua. I did not work in Europe, because untouched territories almost no longer exist there, and evidence of human intervention and pollution is everywhere. On the other hand, I travelled all over Asia, through the Himalayas, and went three times to the Asiatic parts of Russia. I even travelled a lot in South and North America. Thanks to its national parks, the United States has maintained a strong bond with its natural environment, successfully preserving it. I reached Canada, then I faced the cold of Alaska and the vast frozen spaces of the north of the planet. I made a great journey through Amazonia, and also went to

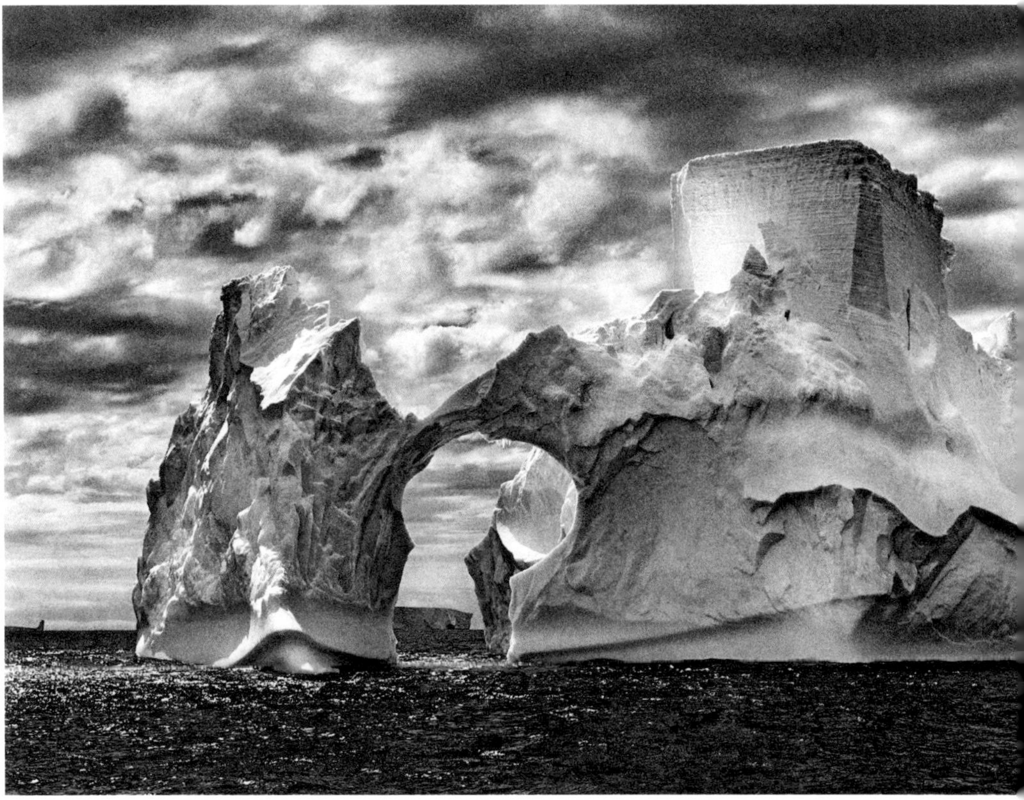

Antarctic peninsula, 2003

Argentina, Chile, Venezuela, to the Diego Ramirez Islands, a Chilean archipelago between Cape Horn and Antarctica. Then I travelled to the Falkland Islands, to South Georgia and to the South Sandwich Islands, which have an active volcano and host the largest existing penguin colony. For me, these are the islands at the end of the world and, as they say in Brazil, they are so far away that the wind turns round there and comes back again. I saw an unbelievable diversity in landscapes, and each journey remains unique.

Those years were fantastic, and brought me great joy. After having witnessed so much horror, I was now seeing so much beauty. Thanks to the team at Amazonas, as I realized these reportages, many of them were published in the international press. In April 2013, two books on *Genesis* were published. Even before I had completed all the reportages, the exhibition of these photos was already planned in many of the great museums all over the world, from London to New York, but also Brazil, Toronto, Rome, Singapore and, of course, Paris. Lélia and I had wanted to pay homage to the planet, and, we hoped, make people reflect on the need to respect it and protect it while there is still time. During my various trips, Lélia has often come to join me. Many times, our breath has been taken away by the majesty of nature, and by all the forms of life that reign there, through the millions of species that inhabit it. In the end, the Earth offered us a magnificent lesson in humanity. Discovering my planet, I have discovered myself and I have understood that we are all part of the same whole system-Earth.

For example, during my very first reportage, in the Galápagos, one day I was watching an iguana, a reptile that, *a priori*, appears to have little in common with our own species. But, looking closely at one of its front feet, suddenly I saw the hand of a Medieval knight. Its scales had made me think of a suit of chain mail, under which I saw fingers similar to my own! I said to myself, this iguana is my cousin. I had before my eyes the proof that we all come from the same cell, each species having then evolved in the course of time in its own way and in conformity with its own ecosystem. The photo of this iguana foot circulates and often appears in the press; if it is able to transmit this idea, I will be happy. In short, with *Genesis* I wanted to recount the dignity and the beauty of life in all its forms and show how we all share the same origins. The encounter with the iguana merely confirmed for me the title we had already chosen for this work: *Genesis*. For me, it has nothing to do with religion, but indicates that harmony in the beginning that enabled the diversification of the species: this miracle of which we are all part.

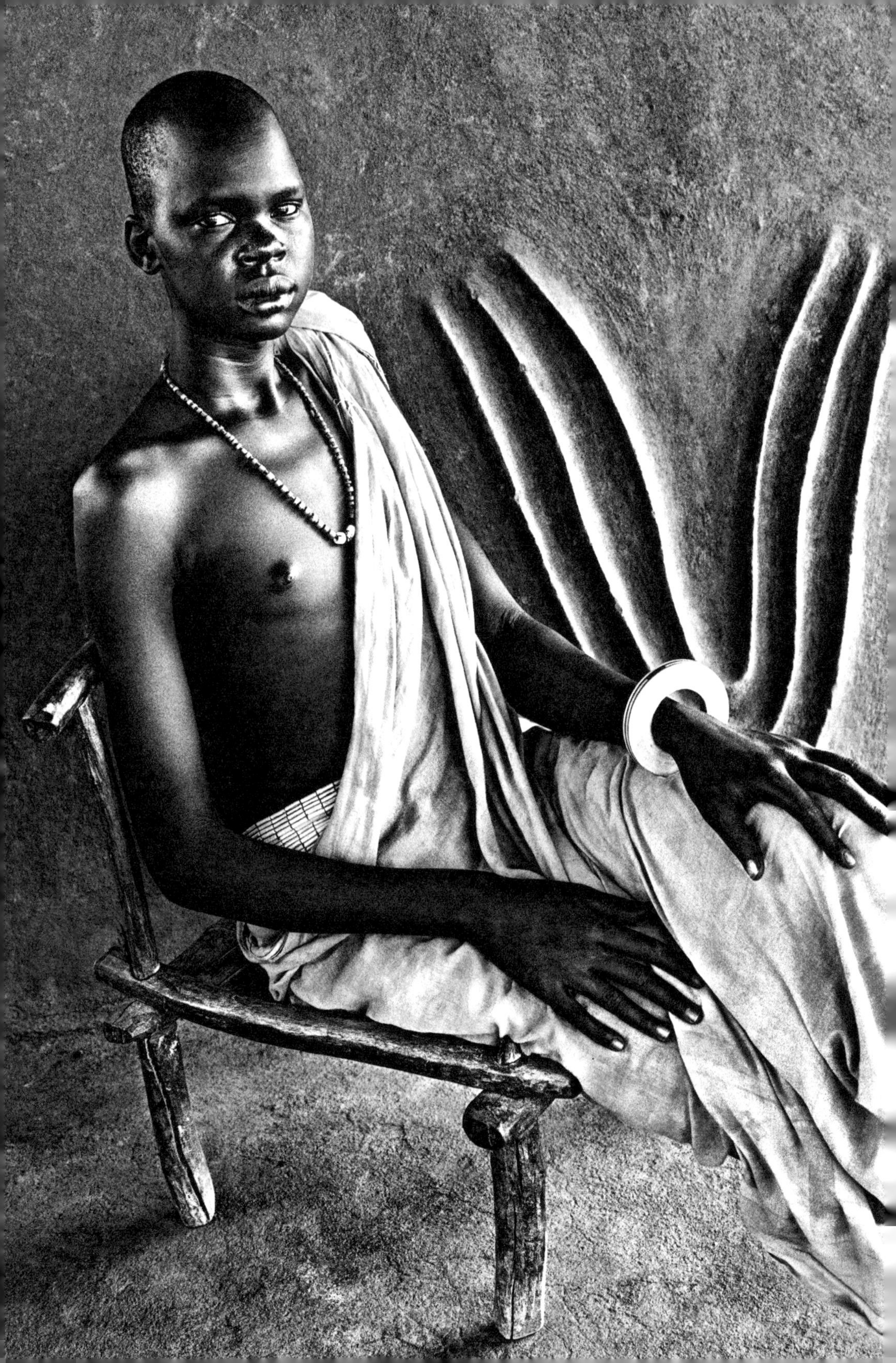

And where are the humans in all this?

Photographing plants, minerals and animals was a novelty in my career as a photographer, which up until then had focused on social issues; a veritable adventure and a great lesson. But for all that, I did not forget about humans. I simply went to discover those who are living as we all lived tens of thousands of years ago.

To rediscover the origins of the human race, I worked with groups who still live in harmony with nature. They are not necessarily the tribes furthest away from our own civilization. For example, I went to Upper Xingu, in the state of Mato Grosso in the centre of Brazil, an area irrigated by the Xingu river, a tributary of the Amazon. It has an indigenous population of about 2,500 inhabitants, who speak Arawak, Caribe and Tupi, divided between thirteen villages, and covers an area about twice the size of Belgium. The discovery of these peoples took place in the 1950s. Nowadays, these Amerindians wear flip-flops, use machetes and, thanks to a solar panel, can receive radio signals. Every afternoon, they can take advantage of radio medical assistance from FUNAI, Brazil's National Indian Foundation, and if their nurse is not enough, a small aircraft is depatched to take them to a hospital. They are thus perfectly conscious of being a minority living on the margins of a majority. They are aware of what is going on in the world and are well acquainted with Western civilization. But they continue to live naked, their existence is still marked by the rhythm of a calendar of rituals of cosmic and mythological inspiration, which give rise to ceremonies that alternate each time between one village and the

South Sudan,
2006

next, and to which all the other members of the community are invited.

I spent three months in this region, during the summer of 2005, to photograph three tribes: the Kuikuro (just over 450 people divided into two villages), the Waura (about 320 people) and the Kamayurá (about 350 people in two villages). I experienced unforgettable moments. With the Kamayurá, I saw the *amuricumá*, a ritual in which the women take power. According to tradition, one day the men left to go hunting and by magic were changed into pigs. Returning to their village, the women beat them and began to treat them like pigs. They took over the running of the tribe, organizing the fishing (fish is their principal food), and so on. During this ritual, which lasts for a month, the women give orders to the men, who are obliged to help them. Then life goes back to normal.

As for the Kuikoro and the Waura, I watched them as they prepared for the *kuarup*, their funeral rite. When I was a child, I used to dream whenever I saw images like these, reading articles in Brazilian magazines describing such ceremonies. I had always wanted to see them. The homage to the dead takes place over an entire year, but the climax only occurs during the last three weeks. Before the final celebration, the whole tribe, men, women and children, leaves to go fishing for a couple of weeks in order to have enough food to feed the three or four tribes invited for the festivities, that is to say one to one and a half thousand people. We climbed on board their pirogues and set off up the lagoon together. Only the elderly stayed behind in the village with the dogs. Beside the fishing grounds, the Indians built fires so that the fish could be smoked as soon as it was caught, to preserve it. It was then wrapped in thick leaves from the trees, mak-

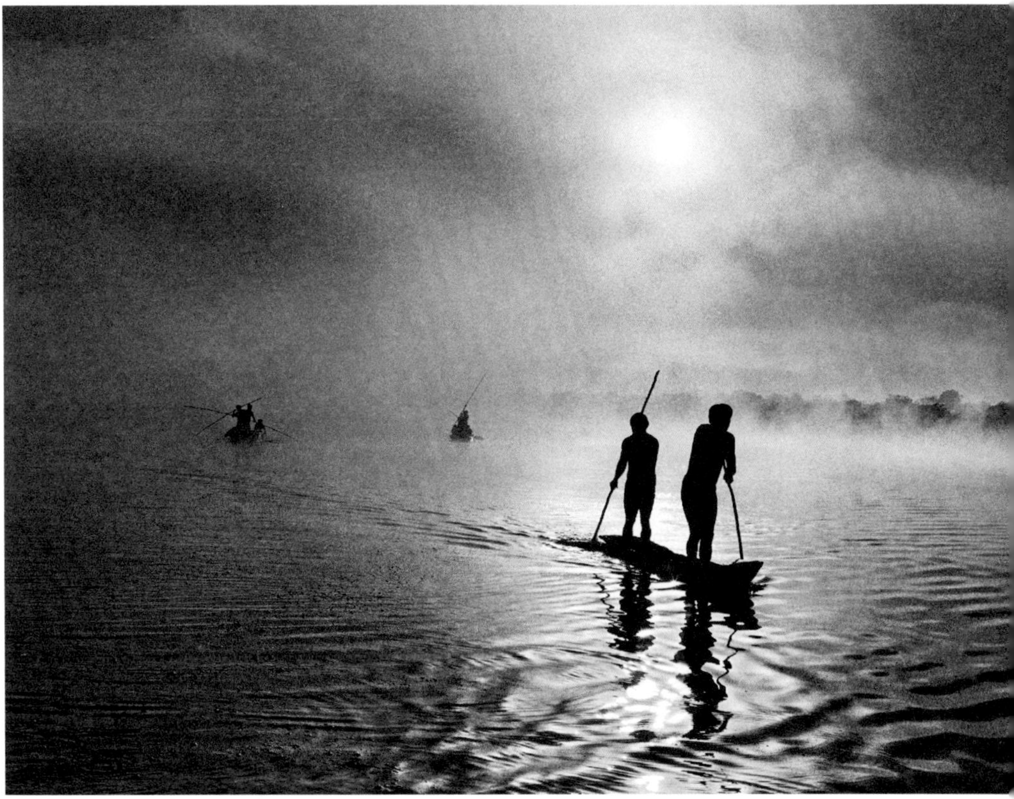

Upper Xingu Region, State of Mato Grosso, Brazil, 2005

ing packets weighing about thirty kilos. When the fishermen thought they had caught enough, we returned to the village. There they had already prepared a supply of flour, the basis of their diet, extracted from manioc root. When the guests arrived, they were received with fish and flour. Each tribe had brought with it spices and salt, obtained by burning certain kinds of leaves.

They then settled themselves in the forest, where spaces had been cleared for them to hang their hammocks. Without exception, all Amerindians sleep in hammocks. When an Indian travels, he is entirely self-sufficient: whether he is

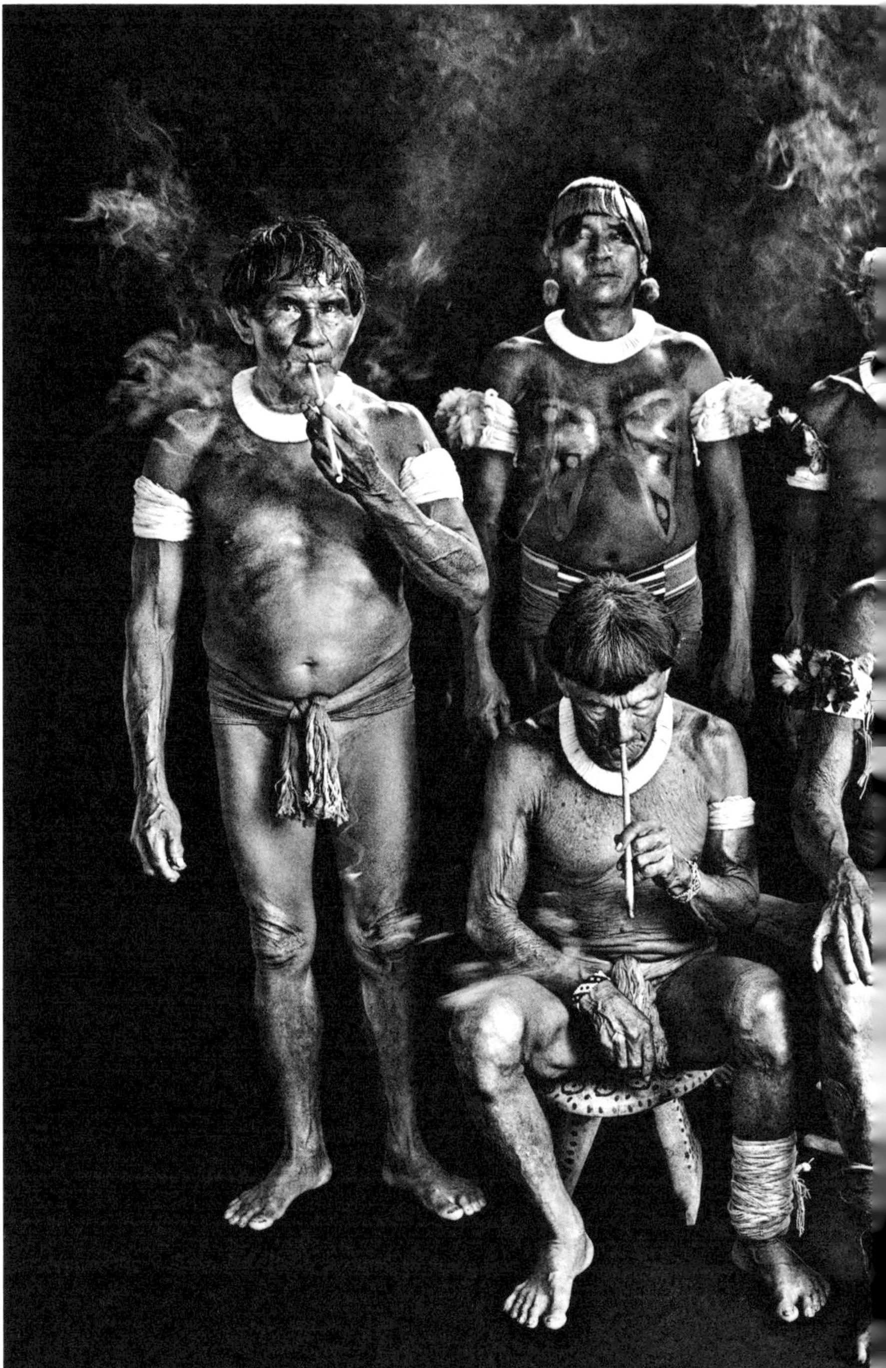

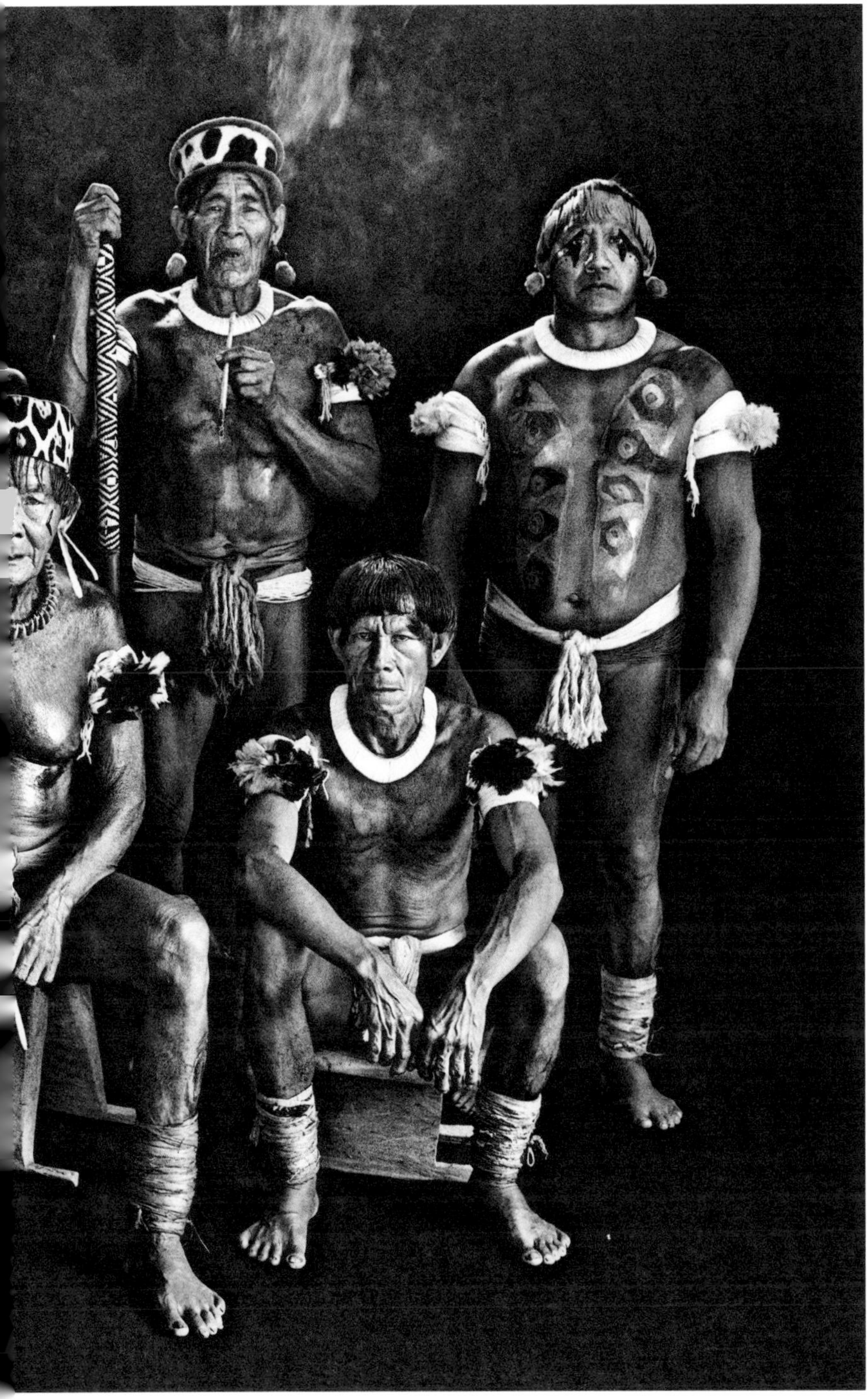

Group of Kamayura shamans, Upper Xingu, State of Mato Grosso, Brazil, 2005

going fishing or hunting, he carries with him his hammock, his bow, his arrows or all his fishing equipment: the Indians know the meaning of essential. I also slept for all those nights in a hammock, I could sleep in one for my entire life (in fact, there are several in our apartment in Paris). Brazilians have adopted this element of indigenous culture and now millions of people sleep in hammocks, especially in the north and northeast of the country.

The great celebrations of *kuarup* are really beautiful. They take their name from a tree supposed to represent the relative who died a year before. During a ceremony presided over by shamans, some men cut down a kuarup tree and take the trunk, which symbolizes the deceased, into the middle of a space with all the participants sitting around it. One by one, they bring as an offering everything the dead person loved when still alive. Then, weeping, they dance around the tree trunk. It is a way of giving back to the deceased the love that he bestowed during his life. He also receives the happiness he brought to those around him, and, at the same time, is shown the sadness of those who remain. Two or three hundred people dance at the same time, while musicians play an instrument that resembles the Alpine horn that is found in Switzerland.

At the end of about ten days of singing, dancing, tears and laughter, when everyone's emotions have been released, a competition is organized for the men (and women), a sort of combat like that found in the Roman circus, in which dozens of couples take part. The aim is not to exchange blows, but to engage in a show of strength. Nevertheless, there are inevitably some casualties. Lastly, the gifts given to the deceased are redistributed among those present, after which the kuarup trunk is taken away and thrown into the water. The mourning ceremonies are then over: the dead person's spirit has been exorcised. These rituals are rich in significance and emotional intensity. It was a great privilege for me to be present.

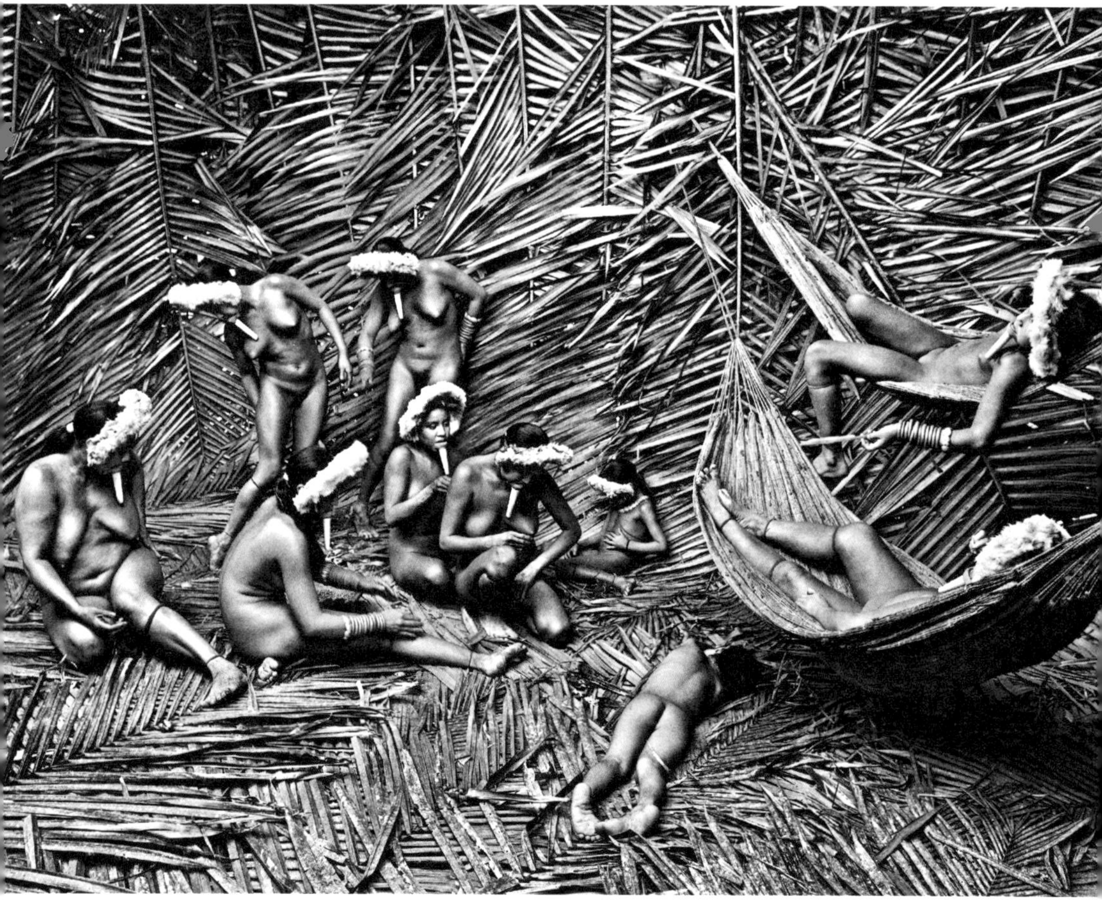

Village of the Zo'é tribe, Towari Ypi, State of Pará, Brazil, 2009

Respect for origins

This series of reportages, like all those I have devoted to the indigenous peoples of Amazonia, involved lengthy preparation with anthropologists, as well as with FUNAI (National Indian Foundation), which reports to the Brazilian Ministry of Internal affairs. FUNAI and the defenders of the indigenous cause, who are its bridgehead, are often criticized. Some accuse them of presuming to know what is best for the Indians, of deciding in their place what should be done for the populations they mean to protect. But undeniably they play an important role with these minorities threatened to a greater or lesser degree. Thanks to FUNAI which is mainly responsible for this success, Brazil is the only country in the world in which over 12.5% of its territory, that is to say an area one and half times the size of France, is made up of Indian reserves recognized by law.

In the past, some groups in Amazonia were forced off their land. Others, like the tribes in Upper Xingu approached for the first time during the 1950s, have seen migration towards the towns near their reserves, in Mato Grosso. Being hunter-gatherers, they had no knowledge of agricultural work on farms, or even work in towns. They rapidly became what Marxism refers to as the *lumpenproletariat*, or sub-proletariat. Many sank into alcoholism, numerous others died of misery. Some returned to the villages they came from and took up their ancestral traditions again, although not entirely. Nevertheless, they rediscovered their language, their way of life, their culture, their history. They regained control of their own destiny.

Since the left came to power in Brazil in 1995, the situation of the minorities has changed. Many indigenous territories have been demarcated, others legalized. The indigenists sometimes manage to obtain agreement from the government to expel farmers from indigenous lands occupied illegally. In June 2013, I carried out a reportage with Survival International and FUNAI on the territory of the Awas Indians to denounce the invasion of their land by farmers, as well as the theft of their timber. Their territories and their woods also belong to the Brazilian people. In addition, the streams that feed into the Xingu river are polluted by the insecticides and fertilizers used in the huge soya fields farmed close to the park; deforestation has altered the region's ecosystem; finally, the construction of hydroelectric dams further up the river has modified the flow and volume of the waterways. The construction, currently underway, of the huge Belo Monte Dam, on the mid Xingu, poses an enormous threat to the rainforest, the river and the indigenous populations. If the project reaches completion, it will without any doubt be one of the greatest ecological crimes of our time.

Without FUNAI, certain tribes might well have disappeared, for example, the Zo'é tribe, which I visited in 2009 and which then had 278 members. It was a minority belonging to the Tupi-Guarani linguistic group that lived on the Atlantic coast. But the Zo'é settled far from the sea: at some point, a long time ago, they were forced into the rainforest, and they never went back. In the sixteenth century, in their writings some Jesuits mentioned their presence not far from the Amazon. Then they vanished without trace. Recently, they were identified again, unmistakeably, as they wear a highly characteristic wooden lip plug between the lower lip and chin. In 1982, some North American missionaries arrived with the intention of leading these "lost souls" back to God. FUNAI therefore intervened and, with the help of the Federal police, expelled the evangelists, together with everything they had brought with them. Apart from this contact, the Zo'é have lived in isolation, receiving only the occasional visit from white men, as in my case, in a controlled context.

FUNAI authorizes visits only if the Indians agree. Nevertheless, it imposes very strict rules of hygiene, since the Indians have no experience of infectious disease and we risk passing these on to them. In addition, prior to going there, visitors have to undergo a series of tests and they are given a series of recommendations, for example, not to give the children sweets, because their teeth are extremely healthy. If we start to give them our sugars, they will soon have caries. FUNAI also handles negotiations with the tribes and together they decide what we have to give in exchange for permission to come and work with them. They usually prefer presents to money. Some asked for outboard motors, others wanted *misangues*, the small, coloured pearls they use to make their jewellery. We brought these for them. But the Indians had warned us: they didn't want the Chinese ones, which are not so beautiful, they wanted the best, from the Czech Republic!

I spent nearly two months with the Zo'é, together with a linguist, Ana Suely Arruda, from the University of Brasilia, who helped me to enter into contact with them. In time, I made a friend, Ypo. I adored him. We walked together for hours, he was unbeatable in catching snakes, never missing them with his arrows. He was fascinated by my Swiss army knife. But João, FUNAI's official, had advised me not to give them anything. I explained to Ypo that if I gave him my knife, João would never allow me to come back to see him again.

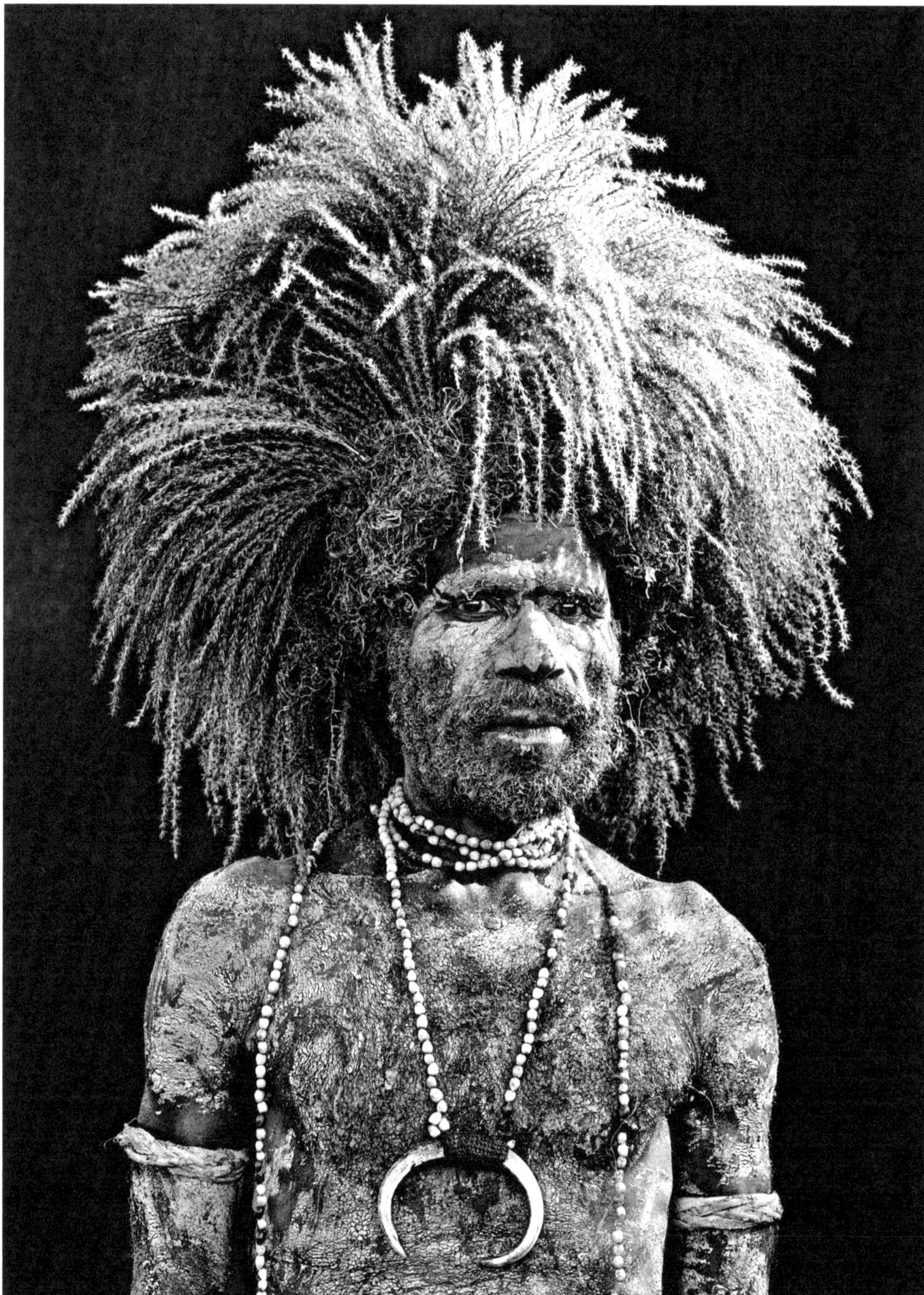

Western Highlands Province, Papua New Guinea, 2008

He replied, "Alright, but when you leave, when you are flying over the forest, throw it to me from the plane. I know where the plane passes, I'll find it". I thought this was incredible. To find anything in that rainforest seemed impossible, but he felt he could do it. I am almost certain that if I had thrown my knife from the plane, he would have found it. Nevertheless, I didn't. No one has the right to decide what is good for them, but I decided to respect FUNAI's rules. My task was not to judge, and certainly not to carry out an anthropological survey.

In 2012, shortly after my visit, the Zo'é disappeared. They left their villages, with the exception of the elderly, who could no longer walk. They covered 300 kilometres of rainforest to go and see a city and visit that world which they had heard the missionaries and the occasional white man, like myself, talk about. I learnt that in the end they returned home. This time, no one made that decision for them: they had simply preferred to go back to their own way of life.

These people charmed me with their gentleness. Violence was unknown to them, as was fighting. Even more astonishing was they had no experience of lying. I don't know who invented the lie, which civilization, but the Zo'é tribe doesn't tell lies. When there is a misunderstanding, the two adversaries climb onto a tree trunk. Each stands on one side of it and his supporters gather behind him. In turn, both set out the causes of their disagreement. When one puts forward an argument, one of those present immediately intervenes to offer a correction or clarification, then the other replies, and so on. It's almost like an exorcism. Anyway, the misunderstanding ends in agreement and provides an opportunity for a celebration of reconciliation. In this tribe, "no" doesn't exist, nor does repression. I realized this one day, at my own expense, while I was photographing a group of women and children, including one kid who wouldn't stop messing around. At a certain point, exasperated, I begged Ana Suely to ask the mother to calm him down. She talked to the mother, then, somewhat embarrassed, explained: "Sebastião, they don't know what a reprimand is, they don't know how to say no".

All these people who live naked, like at the dawn of humanity, were perfectly aware of what a camera was. They posed in front of it and, through my work, were proud to feel themselves observed and taken into consideration. They were familiar with their own image, for they saw it reflected in water. What is more, when the evangelists had been expelled from the tribe, the Zo'é women had persuaded FUNAI to leave them an object that those Westerners had allowed them to discover and which they no longer wished to do without: the mirror. As for the rest, they have nothing to envy in our world. They have their own pharmacopoeia: they know about antibiotics and anti-inflammatories. We have industrialized the process and developed synthetic products, but they have mastered all the basic principles. The laws of ballistics hold no secrets for them. They attach feathers to their arrows in different ways depending on whether they want to shoot them long distances or at a specific target. We have mathematicized these practices, but they are based on the same knowledge. Both sexes are polygamous and, thanks to an extremely precise lineage system, avoid consanguinity nevertheless. In other words, they possess scientific knowledge and have elaborated a social system. They don't believe in a god, or refer to any transcendental beliefs and they don't practice any religion, although they celebrate rituals and possess great wisdom. They have a strong sense of solidarity, they are loving, they love their children: they are similar to us in every way, but they simply live as we lived ten thousand years ago. What distinguishes us from each other is the relationship with nature.

Like all the peoples that I met for *Genesis*, they have a perfect knowledge of their own environment. Following urbanization, we no longer know the names of trees, we no longer pay attention to the mating season of animals, and have become unaware of nature's cycles. In Europe, the exodus from the countryside occurred over several centuries, while in Brazil, in just fifty years, the population has changed from being 90% rural to 90% urban, a brutal transformation that has cut man off from nature. But this phenomenon can be seen all over the world.

My digital revolution

In the middle of *Genesis*, I changed from analogue to digital photography—a true revolution—especially as, for this project, I had already faced two great challenges: to photograph things I had never photographed before, landscapes and animals, and to change the film format. I went for a medium format 4.5x6 in order to obtain a better quality of image in large-scale prints. Between 2004 and 2008, I used a Pentax 645,[1] whereas before I worked in a 24x36 format with my Leica cameras. The medium format does not only mean a change in the size and weight of the camera, but it alters the entire depth of field. Everything works differently than in 24x36. You have to use the aperture much more. The size and proportions of the negatives are not the same. The 4.5x6 is much squarer. I obtained horizons that were too often oblique, something that had never happened to me in 24x36 with the Leicas.

With my 24x36 cameras, I used Tri-X 400 film. In a medium format, I found myself using Tri-X pan 320, another version of this film.[2] It is a film conceived for studio photography and wedding photos. With a certain kind of light it was fine, but with others, like the dense greens of the rainforest, it was very difficult. So I found myself with a film

1. The 4.5x6 format negatives measure 41.5x56 mm. The 24x36 format takes its name from the size of its negatives, which is 24x36 mm.
2. There are two versions of the Kodak Tri-X film, 320 and 400 ISO. The Tri-X 400 is made for the 24x36 and for the medium format 120, whose length only allows 16 exposures with the Pentax 645. The medium format 220 has 32 exposures. In 220, the 320 ISO version was the only one available. It was produced by Kodak until 2010.

three times the size and inferior in quality, because with the increase in the cost of raw materials, their composition had changed. As the cost of silver gradually rose, the amount of silver salts contained in the emulsions decreased. The range of greys thus became much poorer. With Imaginoir and Philippe Bachelier, the two Parisian laboratories I work with, we had to evolve a particular development process. Imaginoir altered the traditional chemical formula of the Kodak D76 developer, while Philippe and I also discovered a developer (Calbe A 49) in the middle of Germany. In short, it was extremely delicate and complicated.

September 11 turned the lives of photographers upside down. Travelling with film became a nightmare after the installation of electronic security barriers in airports. When film passes through X-rays three or four times, the range of greys is badly affected. Little by little, as I went ahead with my reportages, the airports reinforced their security systems. A week before leaving, Jacques and I began to worry. I was about to go to the other side of the world in difficult conditions to capture images and, at the same time, I knew that there was no salvation for my films. I always left with a small case containing 600 rolls of film, in other words 28 kilos of hand luggage that I kept with me in the plane. Each time, I had to argue with the security guards, even though *Paris Match* and Kodak had provided me with letters explaining the problem and requesting a manual check. But how many planes have I missed because these security personnel didn't want to listen and I had to go directly to the airport management? In the end, it became so complicated that I was on the brink of abandoning my beloved photography altogether. In the meantime, however, digital photography had made great progress. So I began to consider it.

Philippe Bachelier, my photographer friend and a great expert in digital images, assured me that it was possible to obtain pictures of extremely high quality with the latest reflex cameras. In June 2008, we began to carry out some comparative tests. Canon had lent me its most sophisticated camera, the 1Ds Mark III. In view of the excellent results, I realized I could change to digital after all. The main problem was the conservation of the archives on hard disc. For almost two years, Philippe and I had been working like mad, together with the Agency's printers Valérie Hue and Olivier Jamin, and then with the Dupon laboratory. Finally, we succeeded in obtaining 4x5 format black and white negatives from digital files.[3] These negatives were of excellent quality and we continued to produce gelatin silver prints from digital film. We thereby avoided problems of conservation which, at the moment, have still not been resolved.

I don't know how to edit, that is to say make my selection of images, on a computer screen. I just can't do it. I have never worked on a screen and the changeover to digital has not altered the way I operate. The only difference is, instead of carrying a small case weighing 28 kilos, I now carry about 700 grammes of memory sticks, which run no risk from X-rays. I never take computers or hard discs on assignment. I photograph simply by looking into the viewfinder, as I have done all my life. When I bring my memory sticks back to Amazonas, we print the contact sheets on inkjet paper and I look at them with a magnifying glass, as I always have done. Then, Adrien Bouillon makes some proofs measuring 13x18 cm. I make an

3. Negatives of 4x5 inches (about 10x12 cm).

initial selection with Françoise Piffard and, co-ordinated by Marcia Mariano who is in charge of managing contact with the labs, Valérie and Olivier print them in 24x30 cm format. All that I have changed in passing from film to digital is the support. My language is the same. But the great difference is that the quality of the print is infinitely better.

Before, it was difficult for me, preferring to work with natural light, to obtain perfect prints. In the enlarger, there were only a few seconds to carry out the masking, but you never obtained a perfect print. This is now possible. The printers can work on every part of the image. Another advantage is that I can work in very low light and increase the sensitivity. If I had worked with a digital camera twenty years ago, I would have twice as many photos. At least 95% of those I took in interiors were lost, because I was photographing people in motion, in action. Shooting at 1/4 or 1/2 a second has rarely allowed me to obtain a clear image. With today's equipment, I have succeeded.

And then, it pollutes less. Before, fixative was thrown away every day. How many thousands of litres were poured away! With computers and inkjet prints, pollution is much reduced.

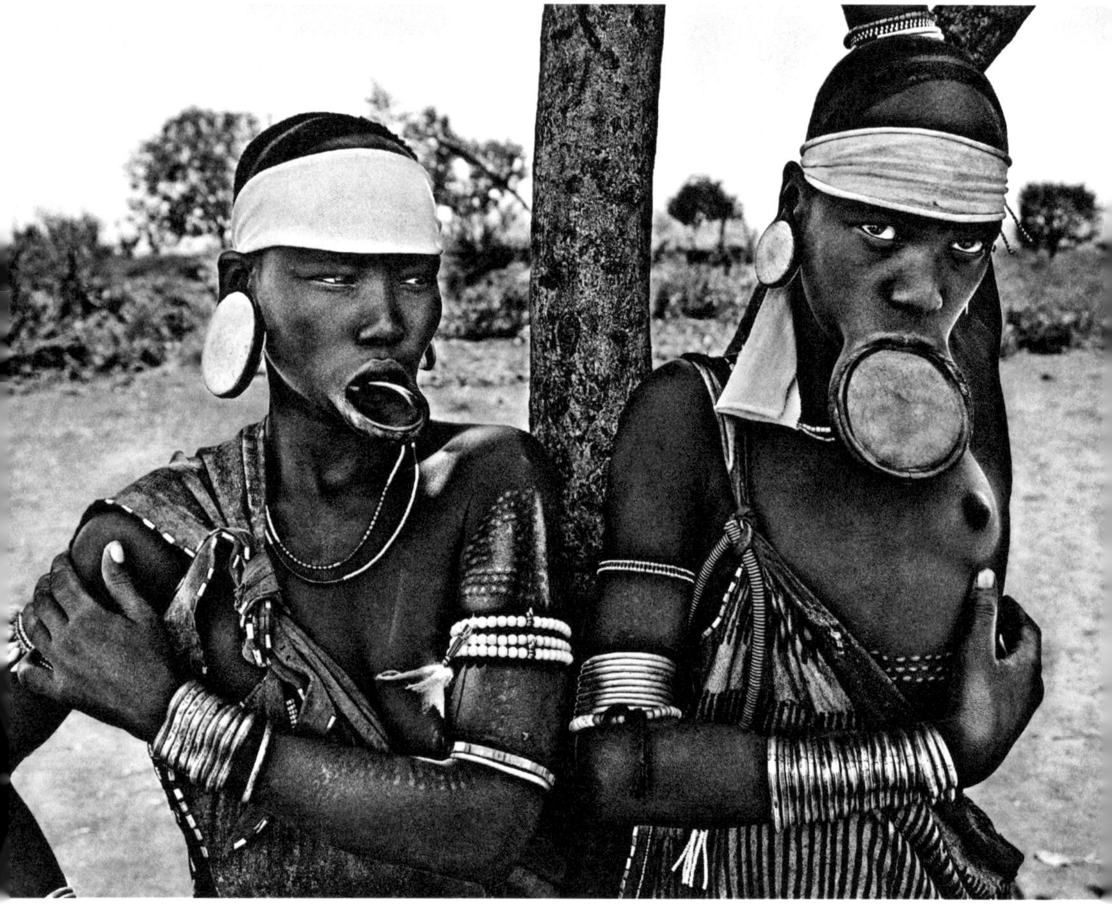

Mursi and Surma women, Ethiopia, 2007

In the footsteps of the Queen of Sheba

My reportage on the Ethiopian highlands, from the town of Lalibela to the Simien Mountains National Park, was one of the first I realized with a digital camera. It is perhaps the most beautiful and most interesting journey I have made in my whole life. It represented a challenge: almost no one ventures into these almost unknown territories. I was told they were dangerous. Would I be up to it physically? What if I broke a leg, or was bitten by a snake, who would help me?

In the autumn of 2008, I covered at least 850 kilometres on foot across mountains it is impossible to cross in any other way. For fifty-five days I walked not on roads, but only on paths that were not man-made, but traced through repeated use over the centuries. No precise topographical survey exists and, on three occasions, I ascended above 4,200 metres. At the lowest point, we were around 1,000 or 1,500 metres. While I climbed these peaks, I felt I was going back through history.

I had been advised not to trust the indigenous people. On our departure, I and my little caravan of mule-drivers and the donkeys carrying our supplies were protected by two guards armed with Kalashnikovs. Apart from the children who were terrified at seeing a white man for the first time, and a bald one at that, we were so warmly welcomed everywhere that I was soon able to dismiss our guards. Every two days, thanks to my satellite phone, I contacted Géo-Decouvérte, a Swiss organization specialized in conceiving itineraries for scientists. Together, we had meticulously planned my journey.

When I communicated my GPS position to them, they told me whether or not I was heading in the right direction.

Malcolm, my Ethiopian guide, was an extraordinary man—how we laughed together! An agricultural engineer, who knew my Swiss friends at Géo-Decouvérte, he had never been along this route before. He was the expedition leader and an Ethiopian marathon runner also accompanied us. He carried the photographic equipment, as the donkeys would have shaken it about too much. I carried the camera bodies. We also carried some solar panels, very light and flexible, to recharge my camera batteries and some storage batteries. Whenever we stopped in a village, I recharged the batteries of my cameras, phone and electric shaver—I have shaved my head every day since 1994, because I caught too many parasites in the years when I had a beard and wore my hair long. In other words, as far as energy was concerned, I was entirely self-sufficient.

We covered 20 to 30 kilometres a day, often over loose stones, in temperatures that were freezing at altitude and warmer at 1,500 metres. We saw snow and crossed lands that were very barren. Sometimes, for four or five days we hardly washed. And when we found a stream, everyone jumped into the water. We then allowed ourselves five or six hours rest, washed our clothes and, when they were dry, set off again. It was hard, but at the same time, it was a good life. On certain paths, we knew that I was the first Westerner to go there: the local people did not recall ever coming across one. It was like diving into an incredible Judeo-Christian world that was surprisingly like the Church described in the New Testament.

The Ethiopians are Semites and consider themselves to be the descendents of the Queen of Sheba and King Solomon. They are proud to be the only people in Africa who have

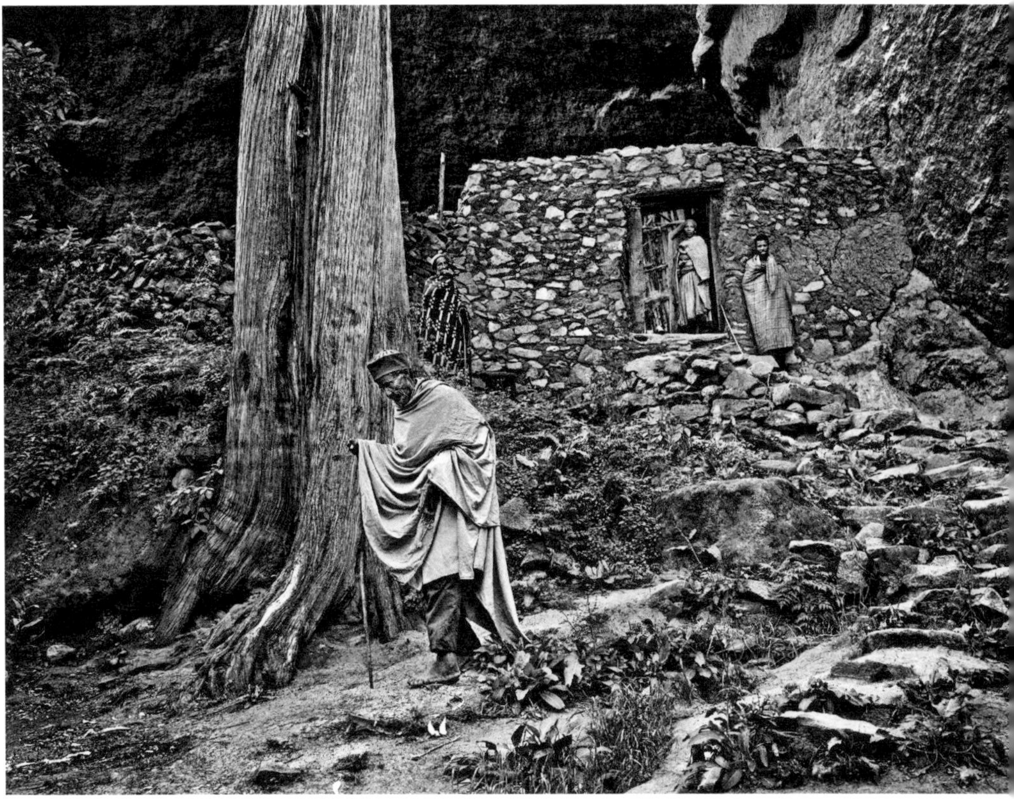

Makina Lideta Maryan Christian church, Ethiopia, 2008

never been colonized. Many Ethiopian Jews, the Falasha, left to go to Israel in the 1980s. Over 60% of the population is Christian (and 30% Muslim). Christianization goes back to the fourth century, with the conversion of King Ezana. In this country, a Monophysite[1] Christian tradition lingers, on the margins of other eastern Orthodox communities. With these believers, I had the sensation of going back to the roots of the Christian tradition.

1. The Monophysites believe that Christ has a single divine nature, as opposed to believers in his two natures, divine and human.

Two or three times, when we arrived in a village, exhausted, the women came to meet us. They took off our shoes and, with a little water, washed our feet. Then they stroked them and kissed them. We felt like Christ in the scene from the Gospels,[2] it was very moving. Every time, we received gifts, food and other presents. We lacked for nothing throughout our journey. We had loaded our eighteen donkeys with pasta, cereals, tins of tuna, processed cheese and other foods that would last for several months because we did not think we would find anything en route. But everywhere we were greeted like honoured guests. I encountered a people who were generous and very touching.

I witnessed rites celebrated in troglodyte churches that took us into the heart of the earth and the dawn of time. Their masses are like a long litany recited in Ge'ez, the liturgical language of Semitic origin uniting all the Abyssinians, who speak two hundred different dialects. It was a magnificent experience, even though I was well prepared. On the other hand, this journey revealed an incredible truth that I would never have imagined: the fertile soils that fed the Egyptians, whose history we have all read, re-read and studied, came from the mountains of Ethiopia. The civilization of the Pharoahs, which lies at the origin of our own civilization and our religions, flourished thanks to the soil of the Ethiopian highlands. It seems amazing, but nevertheless I discovered there the secret of the fertility of the Nile.

Its silt originates in these mountains, thanks to the erosion of their peaks that fall into the surrounding valleys,

2. In the passage in St John's Gospel known as the *Anointing at Bethany*, describing Mary of Bethany washing the feet of Jesus.

forming canyons as big and deep as those of the Colorado plateau in the United States. Carried by the rains, the soil ends up in streams that flow into the Tekezé River, the largest tributary of the Blue Nile which, at its confluence with the White Nile in Sudan, becomes the Nile itself. Before these great canyons, I wanted to express my gratitude—gratitude for all the populations who gave us our humanity, for their contribution to a history that made me dream so much in childhood. It was very moving to touch with my own hands the part that this soil and these stones have played in the destiny of the planet. I understood the extent to which minerals all have their place in our world. Touching this earth, I told myself, it is a piece of me too. We are both part of the same planet, we are both involved in the same history.

I finally came to the conclusion that there is not much difference between me and this earth, just as there isn't much between me and the iguana in the Galápagos. *Genesis* has taught me that everything is connected and everything is alive. *Genesis* is my love letter to nature, and it certainly hasn't made me forget human beings, because they are also part of this magnificent nature.

A world in black and white

Although I turned to nature for *Genesis*, I did not give up black and white. I do not need green to show trees, or blue to show the sea or sky. Colour doesn't interest me much in my photography. I have used it in the past, essentially in assignments for magazines, but for me it represents a series of disadvantages. Firstly, before digital came into existence, the parameters for taking shots in colour were very rigid. With black and white film, it is possible to carry out overexposures of several diaphragms and then correct the photos in the lab, until you obtain exactly what you experienced the moment the shot was taken. With colour, this was impossible.

In the case of analogue photography in colour, I resorted to slides. We placed them on a light box to view them and kept only the most successful. The problem with this procedure is that the sequences are broken and I found this very annoying, while in black and white, you work with the film, which is reproduced in its entirety on the piece of paper we know as the contact sheet. The sequences remain intact, including the photos that have gone wrong. In this way, the story maintains its continuity.

When I was editing analogue photos in black and white, I found myself reliving the events with the same intensity as when the images were taken. I remember that I again felt ill, exhausted, while editing the contacts for one of my reportages on *Other Americas*, during which I had contracted hepatitis (at the time, I still did the developing and printing myself). The notion of continuity, so essential for me, is reinforced by the digital camera, because it records the precise time, to a fraction of a second, of every shot, restoring for me the exact sequence. The contact sheet plays an extremely important part in my photography; indeed, I have kept them all, all the sequences, all the black and white prints realized over more than forty years.

In the days of analogue photography, when I was working in colour using Kodachrome film, I found the blues and reds so beautiful that they became more important than all the sentiments contained in the photo itself. Whereas with black and white and the entire range of greys, I can concentrate on people's intensity, their attitude, their gaze, without all this being disturbed by colour. Of course, reality is not like this, but looking at an image in black and white, it gets inside us, we digest it and, subconsciously, we colour it. Black and white, this abstraction, is thus assimilated by the viewer, who then appropriates it. I find its power extraordinary. That is why, with no hesitation, I chose black and white to render homage to nature. Photographing it like this was the best way for me to show its personality, to allow its dignity to emerge. Adopting the same approach as for humans and animals, to photograph nature, you have to love and respect it. For me, all of this happens in black and white. It is my taste, my choice, but also my constraint and sometimes my problem. Especially when I found myself in the totally white worlds of Antarctica and Siberia in particular. In these environments, if the sun is hazy, hidden by cloud, the images lack relief. So it is necessary to work on the prints to add depth. But in the end, I think the result is really beautiful.

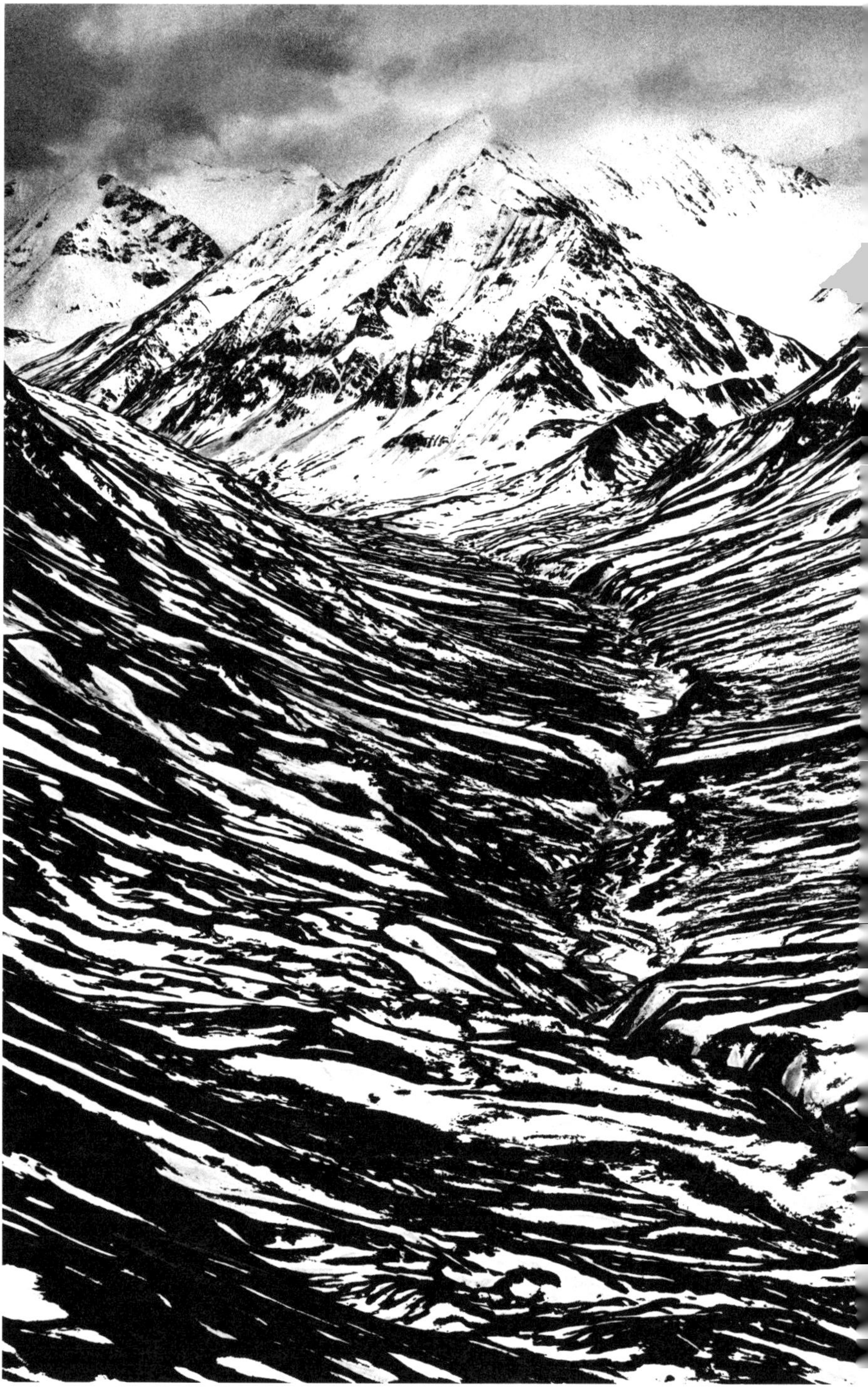

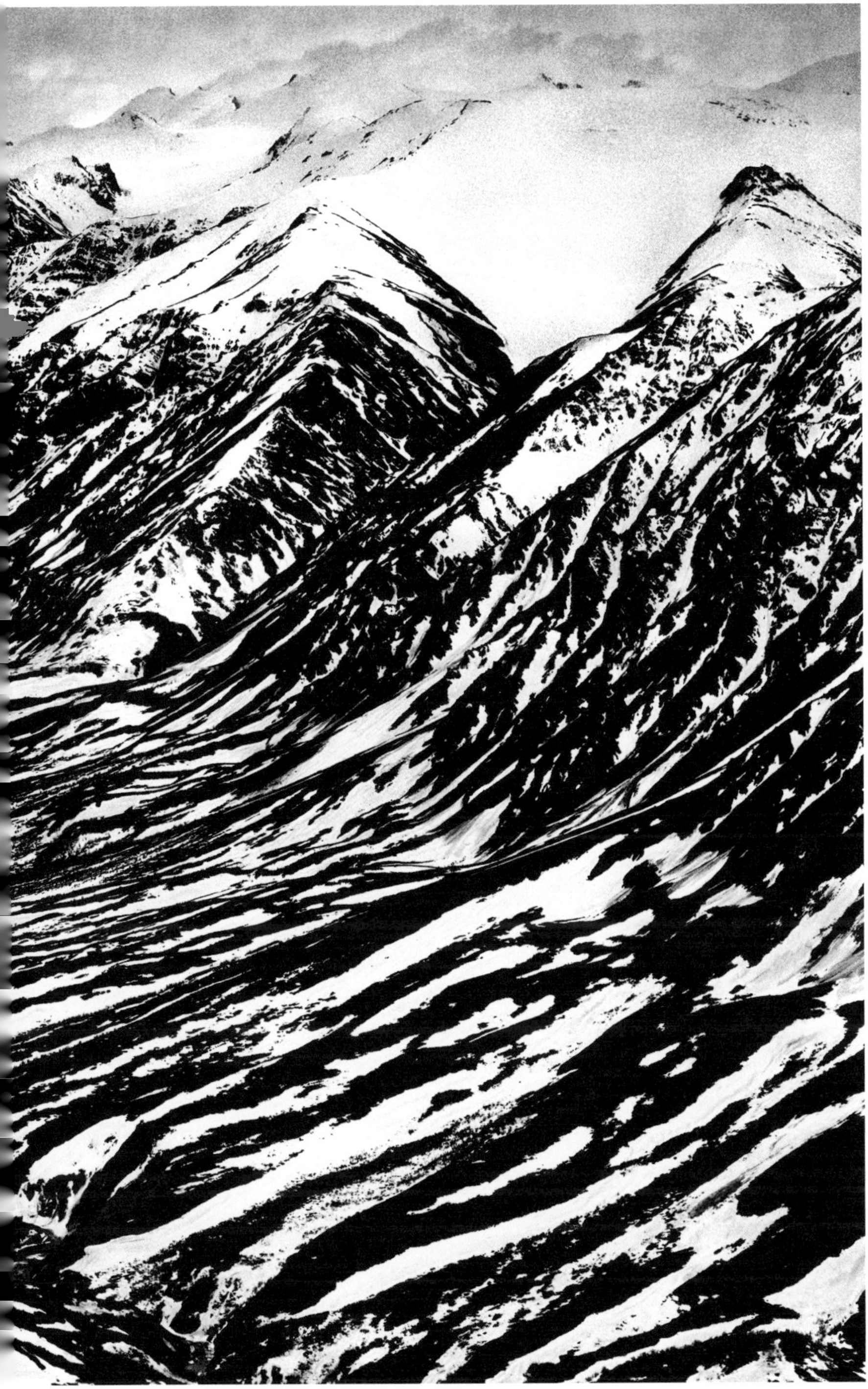

Bighorn Creek, Kluane National Park and Reserve, Canada, 2011

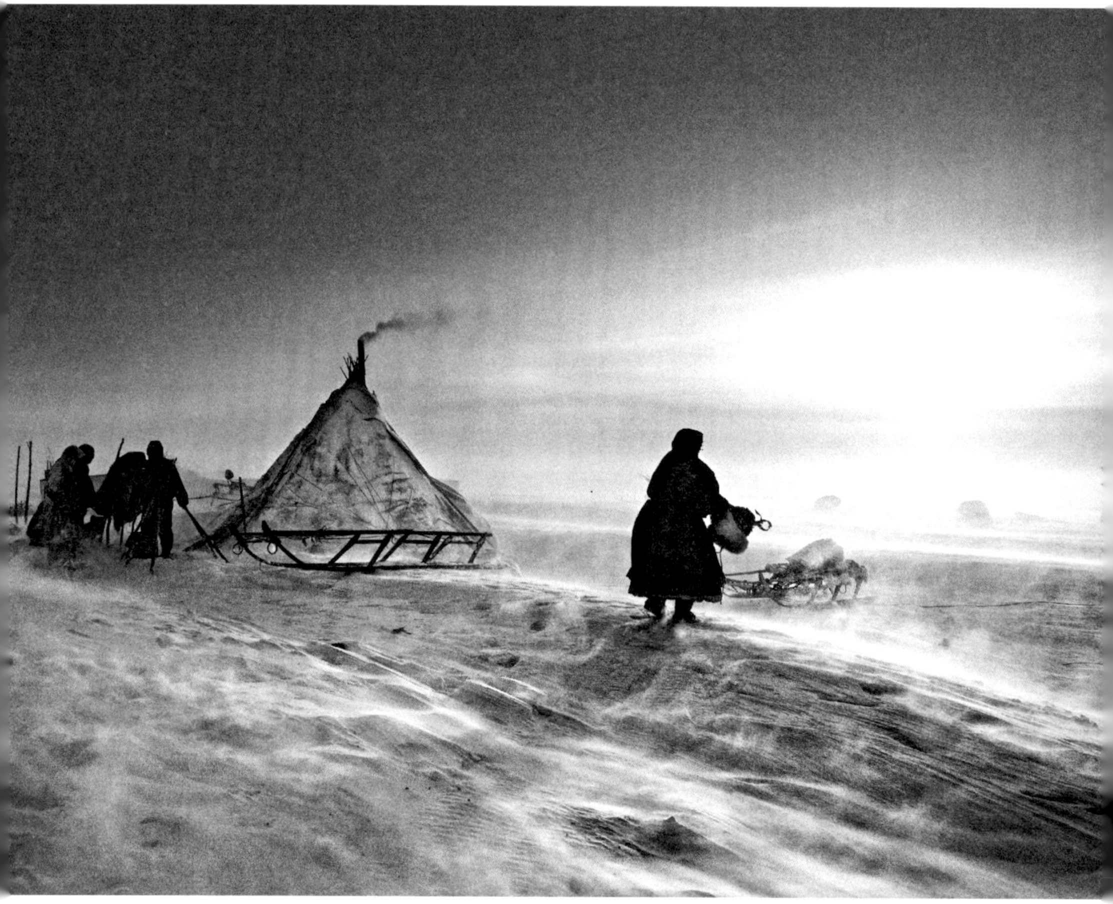

The Nenets and their herds. Arctic Circle, Yamal Peninsula, Siberia, Russia, 2011

The Nenets

In 2011, *Genesis* took me almost to the Arctic Circle to meet the Nenets tribe, the largest ethnic group in Siberia, nomads and reindeer herders. It was bitterly cold, around -30°C or -40°C. The conditions for this reportage were magnificent but extremely difficult, especially for me as I was born in a hot country. Jacques can withstand the cold much better than I can.

We were to be present for the crossing of the Ob, one of the longest rivers in the world, flowing for 5,400 kilometres. By the time we were about to cross it, we had already covered a very long distance in extreme cold. That was the hardest day. It was too much even for the reindeer. But I knew that I could not miss that moment, it was the high spot of our journey. At the same time, we were on a plain that was flat as a board. The sky was completely white, there was little sun, nothing looked easy.

I had planned to take some aerial views, so, in advance, we had contacted a government helicopter, an enormous M18 with a carrying capacity of five tonnes. For reasons of distance and fuel range, I had only forty-five minutes in which to take my photos successfully. So everything had been meticulously prepared. I was extremely tense. Jacques was even more so, and had been ill all night. We had to be sure that the pilot would agree to open the door, that all the harnesses were in place so that I could photograph standing up in the doorway, well secured. Also to be sure that the batteries were working, and that everything would withstand the cold, made all the more intense by the wind. I also wondered if my eye would be up to it, having had a facial paralysis *a frigore* for the last two months. But from the moment the helicopter arrived and I climbed on board, everything went in my favour. In this type of situation, even what is not perfect is part of the game. The strength that derives from having planned for every eventuality and subsequently being in control, provides enormous pleasure in moments of difficulty. You feel yourself carried along by something bigger, something that goes beyond us, but which is inscribed in everything we have patiently constructed beforehand.

The Nenets live in an incredibly harsh climate with the bare essentials. With my customary bad habits, I was afraid that while I was with them I would have nothing. When I got there, I discovered that I had brought, for myself and the journey, far more than they owned. At the end of each day, having covered many miles by sledge, a Nenets pitches his tent, or *tchoum*, made of reindeer skin. Everything he owns is inside it. Next day, he quickly dismantles it and all his belongings are placed on the sledge again. It has to be light in order not to tire out the reindeer. These people who live in cold climates survive with very little, yet their lives are as intense, rich and full of emotions as our own, perhaps even more so, as we multiply our material goods in an attempt to protect ourselves, so much so that we forget to live. We no longer look at nature and other people, we cut ourselves off from our own community. This worries me a lot, as does seeing how in the end almost all the technologies cause us to become more isolated. As the material evolution continues, each of us is able to do more and more alone, in our own corner. The history of humanity is, nevertheless, that of our community, but we, on the contrary, separate ourselves, become individualistic. No one will ever convince me that individualism is worth anything, any more than cynicism is.

It is not a matter of going backwards. No one wants to abandon the comforts of modern life and it would even signify going in the opposite direction to our development, something that has never occurred historically. But we should not lose our points of reference, our instinct, our spirituality. Until now, the bedrock of our lives is our sense of community and our spirituality. This is what I wanted to put into my photos. I have never worked as an individualist, stealing images. Besides, I have been photographing people all my life and I have never had a single lawsuit. I have sometimes photographed people in difficult situations, at the limits, but I have never felt myself to be a voyeur. I've never felt that. On the other hand, with *Genesis*, I realized that I am very, very old.

I have always thought myself part of my group, but transported back 5,000 or 10,000 years. This has comforted me in many of my beliefs. Whether we are talking about the Nenets, the Abyssinians, the Zo'é, the Himba or the Papuans of New Guinea, none of the men and women I encountered are very different from me. We have the same relationship with love, happiness, pleasure, in other words, all the important things in life.

Spending several weeks with peoples who live as we lived at the dawn of time, I have also seen evidence that the great principles on which our world rests existed long before our society became organized. In response to the needs of its masses, industrial society systematized the knowledge and skills acquired since the origins of humanity. I have already mentioned pharmacopeia, the laws of ballistics and practices such as the smoking of fish. To this we can add the knowledge that all these peoples have of nature and the depletion of its wealth, something that Westerners have forgotten for too long. The so-called "primitives" are well aware that after having exploited a plot of land, it is necessary to allow it to rest. I learnt from FUNAI that when the Indians leave a place, they don't return there until a hundred or so years later, once the soil has regenerated.

I did not feel in any way superior to these so-called "primitives". That is why I never felt like an outsider when I visited them. On the contrary, I discovered my equals and, to be honest, they taught me more than I taught them. We had some cultural exchanges and I even made some friends, like Afukaka, the head of the Kuikuro, in the Xingu. I lived for over a month with him and, when I left, I thought he was the most humane being I had ever met in the whole of my life—the best person. It was an amazing experience to be part of his life.

As I have already mentioned, these peoples have a vast knowledge of nature. The Indians are able to sense a jaguar, to see a snake approach, while I saw or heard nothing. They are capable of climbing any tree however high, of walking anywhere barefoot, or almost, while I was having a tough time of it in my ultra-sophisticated walking boots. In the Himalayas, having spent the whole of the previous day in a lengthy descent, I awoke to find that one of my toenails was blue and I was unable to walk for two days. To get moving again, I had to cut the sole of my shoe, and devise a whole new system so that I could continue to follow my local guides.

All men are the same, but our ways of life differ so much that our bodies are no longer the same. Populations living in contact with nature have triangular feet. They are much more agile and their toes grip the ground well, preventing them from slipping. Ours, as a result of being in shoes for hundreds of years, have become long and slender, and can no longer grip. Likewise, with changes in diet, the body changes too. Westerners have become too fat. Even in France, when I first arrived, people were slimmer…

In the end, I can say that the greatest gift I have given myself during these eight years has been the encounter with my own species as it was many thousands of years ago. It has taught me many things that I had mistakenly forgotten in the course of these millennia.

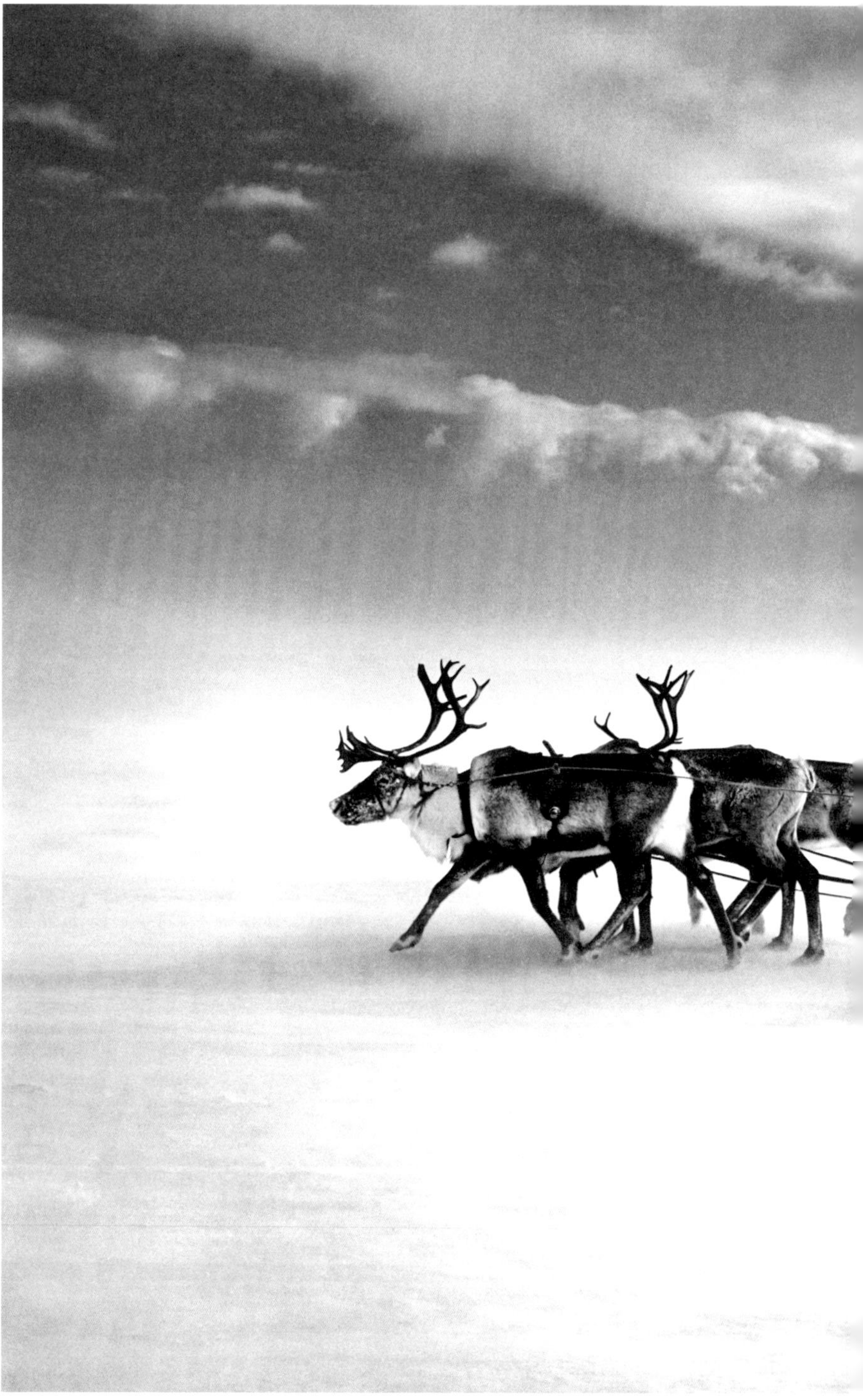

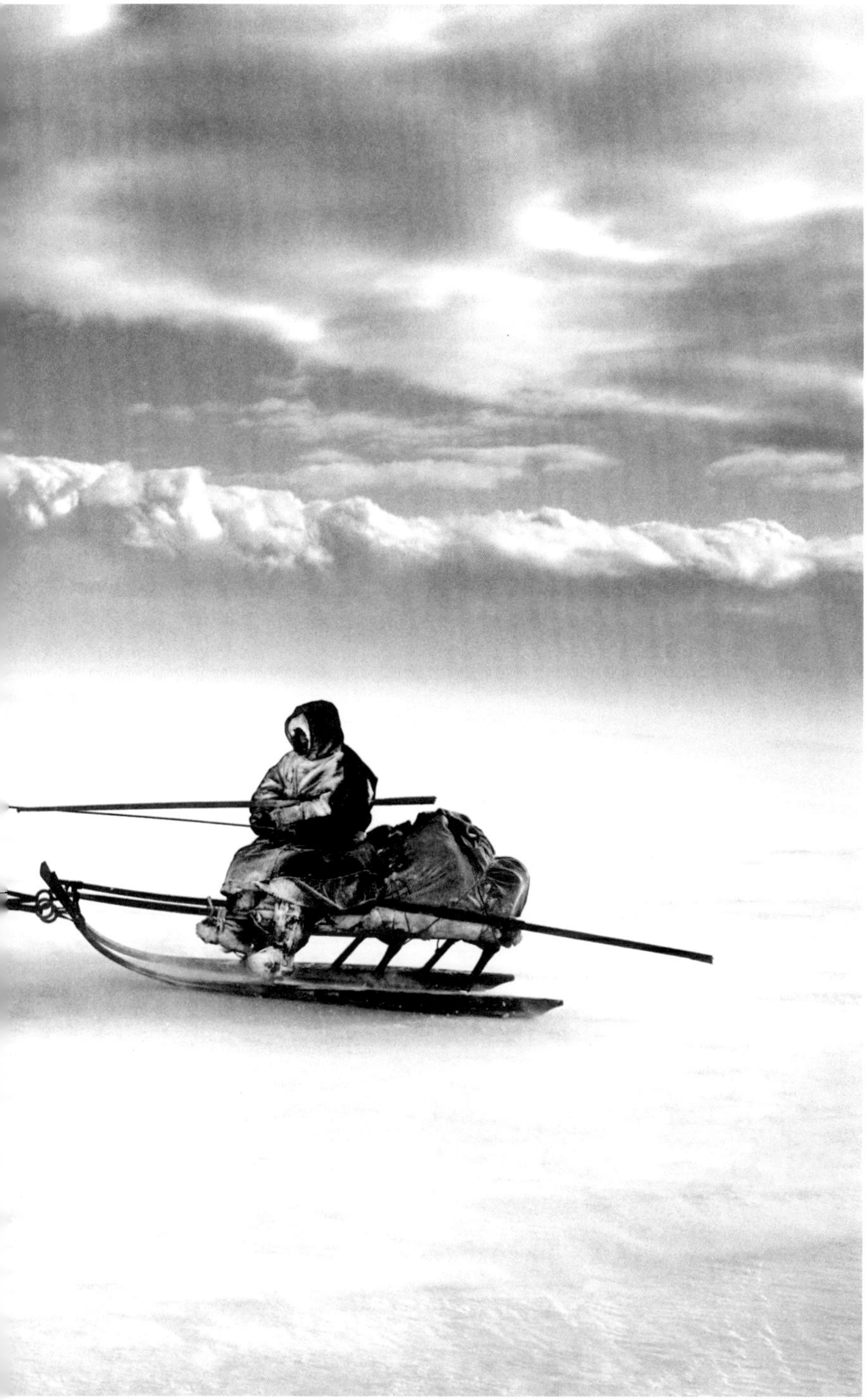

The Nenets. Arctic Circle, Yamal Peninsula, Siberia, Russia, 2011

My own tribe

I was truly lucky to discover photography. And just by chance! Once, my father said to me: "Sebastião, you are a famous photographer, you live in Paris. Do you realize what could have happened if I had sold this farm when you were a kid, in the days of high inflation, when so many others were conned? You would now be driving a tractor in a neighbouring farm, or you might even be living in the shantytown of some big city?" He was right. I have been extremely lucky to be able to experience what I have lived, to have been able to visit more than 120 different countries. It's what I call great consistency, or luck. Everything could have turned out differently. I might have gone to the Soviet Union to finish my studies and perhaps I would never have become a photographer. Or I might have gone to work at the World Bank. I might also have been able to stay in Brazil, have gone into hiding and perhaps got myself killed. Lélia and I might also have separated. And, without her, my life would not have been what it is.

Lélia has given me stability. She has helped me enormously, there is solidarity between us. Every time I am travelling for my reportages, my greatest joy is to get into the final taxi that will take me to the final airport from which I will return home to see my wife and children. Lélia has so often come to meet me early in the morning at Orly, or Roissy. If the plane didn't arrive too early, she would bring Juliano and Rodrigo. I was so touched to find all three of them waiting… Otherwise, she would organize for someone to come and look after them and, when I got off the plane, there she was. Lélia is the great companion of my life, my partner in everything, in ideas, projects, our family, our work, our ecological crusade.

When we first met, she was 17 and I was not yet 20; since then, we have experienced everything together. The other day, walking down the street, I realized that when we decided, with our group of activists, that we both had to leave Brazil, we were still kids. Afterwards, we missed our country and our families very much. Lélia had just lost her parents, but she left behind in Brazil seven brothers and sisters. For eleven years, I too didn't see my own seven sisters and, when we finally returned to Brazil, my parents, who had been strong and healthy when we left, had become old. Homesickness brought us together, but our life has not always been easy. We have had some epic arguments. We were on the verge of divorce and I don't know how many times have we come close to separating! But we have also shared so many powerful experiences, great joys and great fears. We have made important decisions together. I don't know where I start and she ends. My life is the two of us, our two children, Juliano and Rodrigo, and our grandson Flavio. It is because there were two of us that we have got to where we are now. We know what it is to live in another country without a passport, sometimes to have money and others to have none, and have battled on behalf of our children.

I remember that when we had to enrol Juliano in high school, the very fact that he had a Brazilian surname, that is to say Portuguese, meant that he was automatically earmarked for the technical option, despite his own preferences. Once again, it was necessary to fight to avoid him being pigeonholed. But together, we succeeded in taking all of this on.

I adore my wife. And I find her so beautiful. Lélia is a person who is full of energy, takes such pleasure in life and gives incredible strength to her family. Sometimes, I look at her and I think she's starting to get old! This seems impossible, because my vision of Lélia is still as a young girl. We are truly connected. Our family could have fallen apart thousands of times, but she is always there, and at the moment, in good health.

When he was young, Juliano often accompanied me on my reportages, in Asia, Africa, even in Rwanda, in the difficult situation I have already described. But we have shared some incredible moments; discoveries, encounters and good laughs. He has followed me in my work, which is such an important part of me. He knows all my preferences as far as images and journeys are concerned. It is certainly not by chance that he has become a film director. With the great German director Wim Wenders, he has co-directed a film, *Salt of the Earth*, about my work. Juliano lives in Paris and leads his own life, but we see each other often. He and his son Flavio, a splendid teenager, are very close to us and Rodrigo.

The fact of having a child with Down's syndrome, as I have already said, opened up another world for us. The other day, we went to an open day at the centre where Rodrigo spends his days. As always, it was incredible to find ourselves in the midst of all these people with handicaps and to see our son surrounded by his friends. As a result of mixing with them, they have also become our children. This has given me a different view of the world than the one I had when I was "normal', because I only had a child who was "normal" and I lived in a world of so-called "normal" people. The day our Down's syndrome child was born, we achieved a different level of perception; of life, society and reality. Even my way of walking down the street has changed. Before, I never noticed handicapped people. Now, I have learnt to see them.

For over thirty years, our life, mine as well as Lélia and Juliano's, has also been spent in the world of handicaps. We have experienced solidarity and a lack of it. When Rodrigo was born, some of our close friends distanced themselves. Some couldn't take it and this was very painful. It is understandable, and it is acknowledged that, for example, it is difficult for a pregnant woman to frequent a family with a handicapped child. In any event, it is necessary to understand this, otherwise you become bitter. We also realized that many people don't know what to say, don't know how to behave towards a child who is different, who hugs and kisses you, who dribbles. Fortunately, this is not the case with all of our friends. Some, on the contrary, have become closer.

We have never placed our son in a boarding school. He goes to a centre during the day and comes home in the evening. We take him everywhere, he is always with us and attends all the openings of my exhibitions. Some are amazed, but for us it is natural. He is our son and therefore part of us. And we have also built our life around his. When he was small, we always tried to compare him to other kids, to measure his progress, his development, and we were in despair. One is not prepared for this. At one time, we took him to Cologne to consult a specialist in reconstructive surgery to reduce the effects of Down's syndrome on his face. Just before we got there, we stopped at a service station from where it was already possible to see the city. There, talking together, Lélia and I realized that we were about to make our son undergo a major operation for the sake of appearance. He was going to suffer, but there was no hope that the Down's syndrome would be cured. The operation had no meaning for him, only for us. So we turned round and headed back to Paris. You have to experience certain situations in order to understand them. For a long time, we reflected on Rodrigo's problem, discussed it, until one day we found the solution: there is no solution. He is our son, he is part of us, and that's the way it is. We have to love our son, and love him as he is.

In all honesty, as painful as his handicap is, Rodrigo gives us much joy. As I have already said, he has given us the opportunity to look at the world in another way, to meet people who are different. He has given me such tenderness. Our son has confirmed what they predicted: if you give, you receive more back. If you don't give, you will never receive.

I remember once, I was in a refugee camp in southern Lebanon. Things were very tense. I went to talk with the Palestinian authorities who were in charge of the camp. I was there with the UNHCR, I explained the nature of my work, but every time I took my camera out, a Kalashnikov was trained on me. Until the day when a guy went past, I took his photo and he came up and kissed me. He had Down's. So I thought, the solution to our aggressiveness would perhaps be to carry out genetic modification of the famous chromosome pair 21 which, in those with Down's, has an extra chromosome. Because they totally lack any form of aggression. They sometimes get angry, but the anger is directed at themselves, never at others. At any rate, I have never seen it, either in our son, or any others I know who are affected by Down's syndrome.

Every year, we organize two parties for Rodrigo's birthday: one in Brazil, in summer, the other in Paris, in autumn.

We invite Rodrigo's handicapped friends, their families, and then our other friends. It is an opportunity for two worlds to meet and to allow the so-called normal people to discover one of the realities of handicap of which they were often unaware. They thus discover a different world, but one in which much happiness reigns. They realize that the encounter with this world is much easier than they thought. We have lots of laughs with Rodrigo. He draws very well, and loves to draw for hours on end. He has an undeniable artistic sense, a true appreciation of colour. One of his friends plays the piano wonderfully. Their talents are independent of their handicap. Having a son like this gives us a lot, but it also isolates us, as he is always with us. We are rarely invited to bring him with us, and we don't often go out so as not to leave him alone. Some say that Lélia and I go out too little, and that we don't go to the openings… but we live with Rodrigo, and that's what it's like to have a handicapped child. At the beginning it was very hard, but once we rounded the corner, we realized that this was what our life had become. You have to make the best of it.

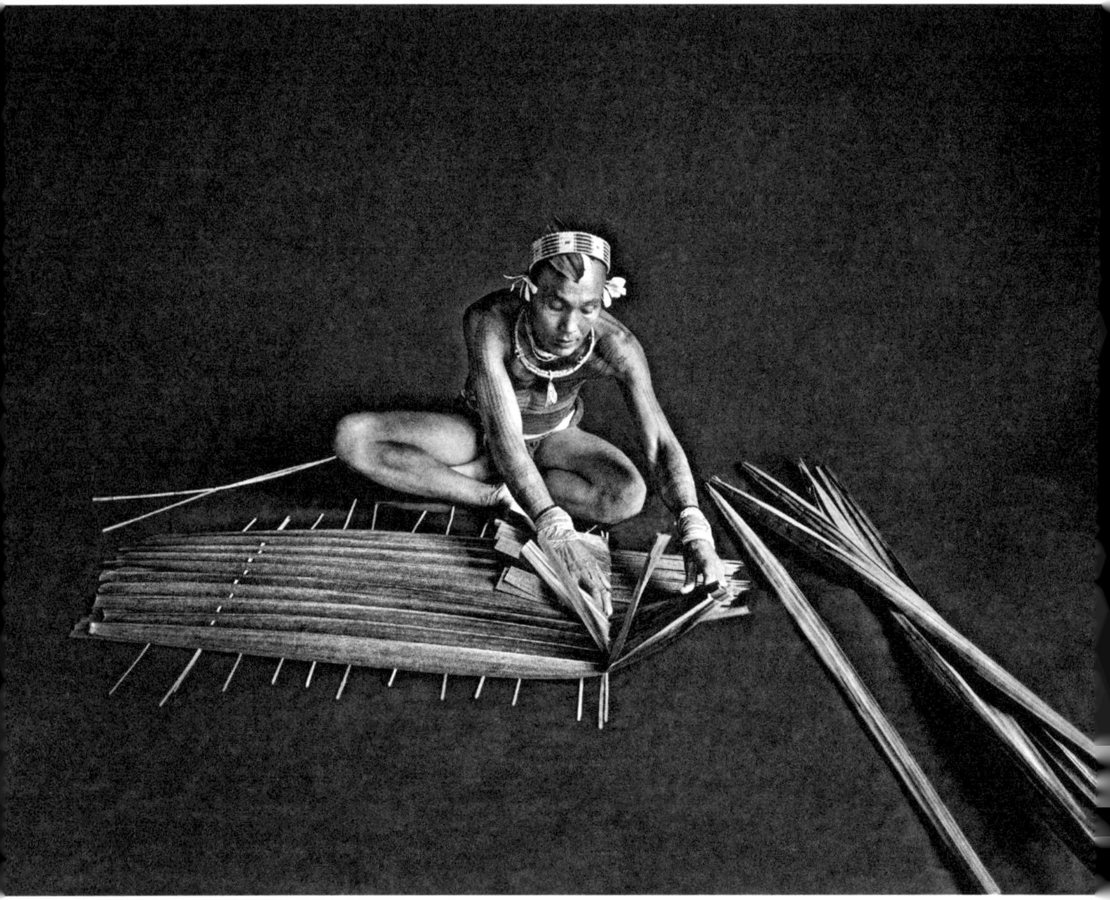

Shaman making a sieve out of sago leaves. Siberut Island, Sumatra, Indonesia, 2008

Conclusion

I was almost 70 when I completed the reportages for *Genesis*. They had physically worn me out. I have faced the rigours of climate, from the coldest to the hottest, the most humid to the driest, and, above all, I have covered enormous distances on foot. In town, we are used to walking on even surfaces, but in the rainforest, with the Indians, you are walking on uneven ground, clambering over tree trunks. Sometimes, some of them are so big that you have to sit on them and then twist round and slide down the other side. You often fall. The Indians never do. The first day of walking in the rainforest, you are exhausted, as you have activated muscles that haven't been used since childhood. And in some cases, muscles I didn't even know I had. To summarize it all, I would say that the mind was blessed and the body punished. After eight years, I was tired, but regenerated inside. For *Migrations*, I had come face to face with everything that is most harsh and violent in our own species and I no longer believed in its salvation. Realizing *Genesis*, I changed my mind.

First of all, I encountered the planet. I had already travelled round the world, but this time I felt that I was entering inside it. I have seen the world from its highest points to its lowest, I have been everywhere. I discovered minerals, plants and animals, and then I was able to look at us, the human race, as we were at the dawn of man. This gave me much comfort, because going back to its origins, humanity is very strong, especially rich in something that we have now lost after becoming city-dwellers: instinct. It is our instinct that enables us to sense and foresee many things, a change of temperature, or other climatic phenomena through the observation of animal behaviour. In reality, we are about to abandon our planet, because the city is another planet altogether.

I have seen what we were before being thrown into the violence of the city where our right to space, air, sky and nature is lost between its walls. We have erected barriers between nature and ourselves. Suddenly, we are no longer capable of seeing, hearing… To watch a bird from behind a window pane and imagine that this bird is the mate of another bird with whom it makes love; that it loves its little ones, that it has built its nest on that tree, that it depends on the wind. We no longer know that the entire structure of its skin and feathers is made to protect it from the sun's rays, rain and snow… We no longer see this, no longer know. Frequenting these peoples who live as we once did, I rediscovered these wonders. I was greatly enriched by the experience. Although I was proud to show in my book *Workers* that man is a creature of incredible ingenuity when it comes to production, I also saw that through our way of life, we have done everything to destroy what guarantees our species' survival.

I do not believe in the existence of a great creator who has ordered nature and the entire living world. I believe much more in evolution and consider myself a disciple of Darwin. I believe certain laws exist, that things are formed through dialectics, accumulated experience, maturation. Nevertheless, not all maturation processes evolve in a positive direction. We are still searching for the explanation of the first moment, but can already scientifically explain the rest. *Genesis* gave me the opportunity to measure the age of my planet. In the Sahara, I saw rocks carved 16,000 years ago; in Venezuela, mountains six billion years old. This adds a different dimension to life. You realize that it is only a brief span.

Genesis made me aware that by cutting ourselves off from nature through urbanization, we have become very complicated animals; as a result of becoming strangers to the planet, we are becoming strange beings. But this is not an insoluble problem. The remedy is transmitted through information and I am happy if I have been able to contribute. I would like to enable it to be understood that the solution to the danger incurred by man and all the species on the planet is not to go backwards, but to return to nature. This is what Lélia and I are doing in Brazil by replanting the forest. Only trees are capable of assimilating all the carbon dioxide that we produce. The tree is the only machine that transforms carbon dioxide into oxygen. The forest assimilates and transforms our pollution into wood, it's amazing. Particularly as once a forest is planted, it is during the first twenty years, while the trees are growing, that the most carbon dioxide is absorbed.

Together with our friends at Instituto Terra, Lélia and I have planted two million trees. We have calculated that, up until now, we have captured 97,000 tonnes of carbon. But everyone can do something, you just have to feel concerned enough. Lélia and I are not wealthy. We took refuge in France and we have worked hard. Fortune has sometimes been kind to us and now we are proud to be able to replant this forest, thanks to the fruit of our work and to everyone who has helped us. But above all, it is thanks to our energy, which derives from a certainty: to turn back towards the planet is the only way to live better. The modern, urbanized world, with its rules and regulations, is constraining. It is only in nature that we can find a little freedom. This is what we wanted to show with *Genesis*, our books and a series of exhibitions around the world.

It is strange the way in which we came to be involved with the environment. Sometimes I wonder, by what sort of luck and the answer is the times we live in. Just as, in the past, the times led us towards industrial changes, and then migrations. To Lélia and I, it will always be important to lead a life that is part of our times, to participate. In the end, when we are asked how we got there, looking back, we realize that it has simply been our life that has led us to where we are now.

My photography is not a form of activism, it is not even a profession. It is my life. I adore photography, taking photographs, holding my camera, choosing my frame, playing with the light. I love living with people, observing communities, and now animals, trees, rocks too. My photography is all of this and I cannot claim that the decisions that make me choose to go here or there are rational. It is a need that comes from deep inside me. It is the desire to photograph that always drives me to leave again, to go and look elsewhere. Constantly to be taking more new images.

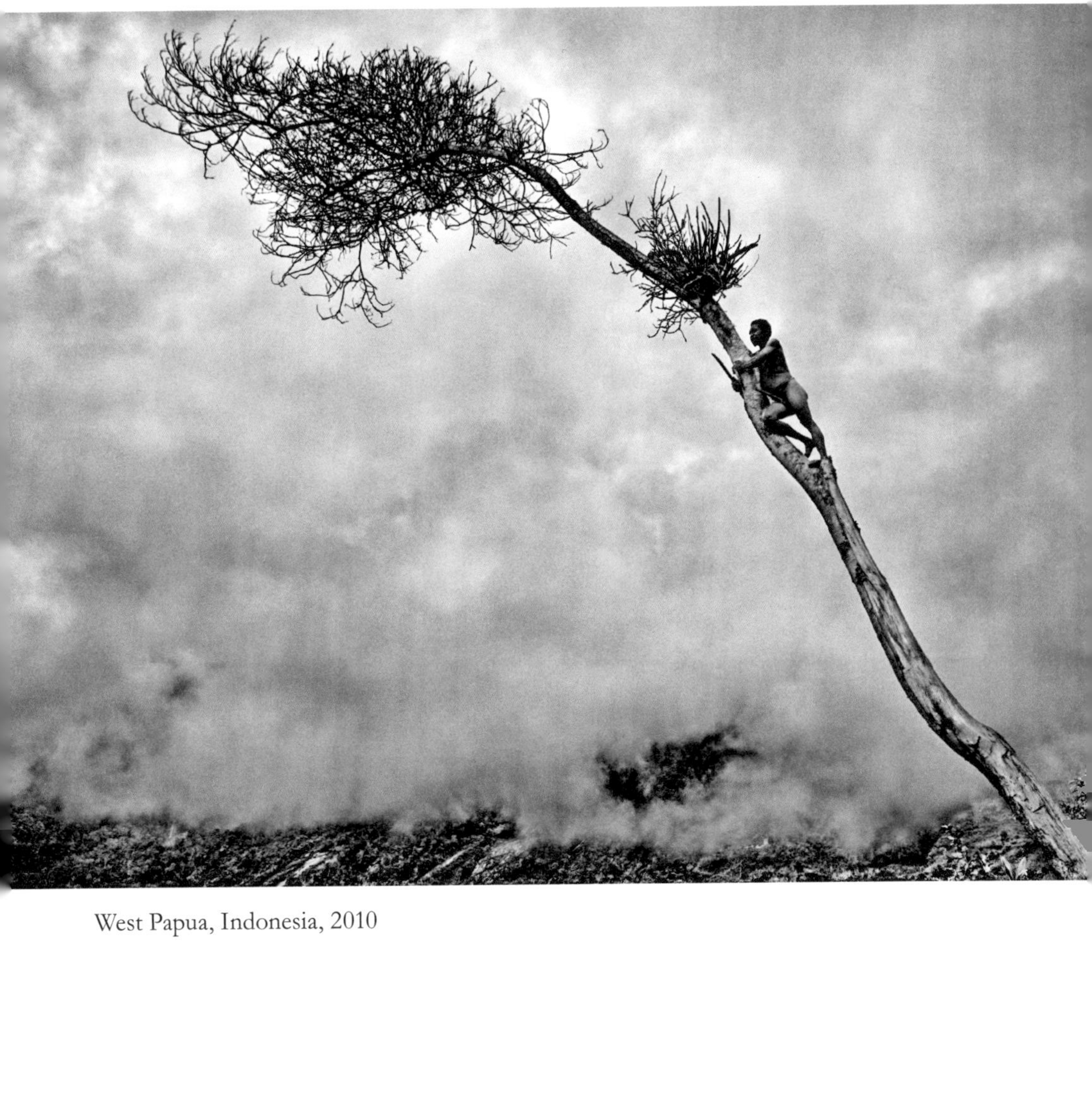

West Papua, Indonesia, 2010

Bibliography

Works by Sebastião Salgado

Sahel: L'Homme en Détresse, Prisma Presse and Centre National de la Photographie, France. In collaboration with Médecins Sans Frontières, 1986.

Other Americas, Pantheon Books, USA, 1986.

Les Cheminots (The Railroad Workers), Comité Central d'Entreprise de la SNCF, France, 1989.

Workers, Phaidon, England, 1993.

With José Saramago, *Terra*, Phaidon, England, 1997.

Serra Pelada, Editions Nathan, France, 1999.

Migrations, Aperture, USA, 2000.

The Children, Aperture, USA, 2000.

The End of Polio, Bulfinch, USA, 2003.

L'Homme et l'eau, Editions Terre Bleue, France, 2005.

Africa, Taschen, Germany, 2010.

Genesis, Taschen, Germany, 2013.

Honors and Awards

1982

Eugene Smith Award for Humanitarian Photography, USA.

Award for continuing the project on the Latin American farmers, Ministry of Culture, France.

1984

Prix de la Ville de Paris et Kodak, for a first photographic book, *Other Americas*, France.

1985

World Press Photo Award, The Netherlands.

Oskar Barnack Prize, for Humanitarian Story, West Germany.

1986

Premio de la Foto Ibero Americana, Spain.

Photojournalist of the Year Award, The International Center of Photography, USA.

Prix du Livre, for *Sahel, l'Homme en Détresse*, Arles International Festival, France.

ASMP Award, USA.

Grand Prix and Prix du Public for the show *Other Americas* by the "Mois de la Photographie", Paris Audio Visuel, France.

1987

Photographer of the Year Award, American Society of Magazine Photography, USA.

Photographer of the Year, Maine Photography Workshop, USA.

Olivier Rebbot Award, from Overseas Press Club, USA.

Jounalistenpreis Entwicklungspolitik, Germany.

Prix Villa Médicis, Ministry of Foreign Affairs, France.

1988
Erich Salomon Prize, West Germany.

Premio de Fotografía Rey de España, Spain.

Photojournalist of the Year Award, International Center of Photography, USA.

The Golden Award, Art Directors Club, USA.

1989
Erna and Victor Hasselblad Award, for life achievement, Sweden.

The Artist of Merit Josef Sudek Medal, Czechoslovakia.

1990
The Maine Photographic Workshop Award for the best Photography Book *An Uncertain Grace*, USA.

Visa d'Or Award, International Festival of Photojournalism of Perpignan, France.

1991
The Common Wealth Award, For Mass Communication, USA.

Le Grand Prix de la Ville de Paris, France.

The Golden Award, Art Directors Club, USA.

1992
Elected Foreign Honorary Member of the American Academy of Arts and Sciences, USA.

Oskar Barnack Prize, Germany.

Art Directors Club Award, Germany.

1993
Prize for the Best Photography Book of the Year, for *Workers*, Arles International Festival, France.

Trophée Match d'Or, for life achievement, France.

The World Hunger Year's Harry Chapin Media Award, for photojournalism, for the book *Workers*, USA.

1994
Publication Award for the book *Workers*, The International Center of Photography, USA.

Awarded Centenary Medal and Honorary Fellowship, The Royal Photographic Society of Great Britain.

Professional Photographer of the Year, PMDA Photographic Manufacturers and Distributors Association, USA.

Grand Prix National, Ministry of Culture and French-Speaking Countries, France.

Award of Excellence, and Silver Award, Society of Newspaper Design, USA.

1995
Silver Medal, Art Directors Club, USA.

Silver Medal, Art Directors Club, Germany.

1996
Overseas Press Club of America, Award, Citation for Excellence, USA.

Auszeichnung, Art Directors Club, Germany.

1997
Prêmio Nacional de Fotografia, Ministry of Culture, Funarte, Brazil.

Prêmio A Luta pela Terra, Personalidade da reforma agrária, Movement of Landless Peasants, Brazil.

1998
Silver medal, Art Directors Club, Germany.

The 1998 Alfred Eisenstaedt "Life Legend" Award, *Life Magazine*, USA.

Prêmio Jabuti, for the book *Terra*, Brazil.

Principe de Asturias Award for Arts, Spain.

1999
The 1999 Alfred Eisenstaedt Award for Magazine Photography. *The Way We Live.* USA.

Prêmio Unesco, Culture category, Brazil.

2000
Medal of the Presidenza della Repubblica Italiana, International Research Center Pio Manzù, Italy.

2001
Degree Honoris Causa, University of Evora, Evora, Portugal.

Honorary Doctor of Fine Arts, New School University, New York, USA.

Honorary Doctor of Fine Arts, The Art Institute of Boston at Lesley University, Boston, USA.

Prêmio Muriqui 2000, Conselho Nacional da Reserva da Biosfera da Mata Atlântica, Brazil.

UNICEF Goodwill Ambassador.

"Ayuda en Accion" Prize, Ayuda en Accion NGO, Madrid, Spain.

2002
Honorary Doctor of Letters, University of Nottingham, Nottingham, Great Britain.

The Art Directors Club 81st Annual Awards 2002, Merit Award for *The final fight against polio*, USA.

2003
International Award of The Photographic Society of Japan, Tokyo, Japan.

2004
Comendador da Ordem de Rio Branco, Brazil.

2005
Gold Medal Award for Photography, The National Arts Club, New York, USA.

2007
Michael Horbach Stiftung Prize, Germany.

2008
Faz Diferença de Globo Prize, Rio de Janeiro, Brazil.

2010
Excellence in the reporting of social issues Award, The American Sociological Association, USA.

NANPA Lifetime Achievement Award, The North American Nature Photography Association, USA.

Save the Children International Prize, Madrid, Spain.

Gold Medal of Honour, the Al-Thani Award for Photography, Doha, Qatar.